It's O.K.
to Be
SINGLE

Other Books from
The Continental Congress on the Family

Make More of Your Marriage
The Secrets of Our Sexuality
Facing the Future: Church and Family Together
Living and Growing Together: The Christian Family Today

It's O.K. to Be SINGLE

A Guidebook for Singles and the Church

Edited by

Gary R. Collins

WORD BOOKS, Publisher

Waco, Texas

First Printing, June 1976
Second Printing, October 1976
Third Printing, March 1977

ISBN #0-87680-858-5
Library of Congress catalog card number: 76-2857
Printed in the United States of America

Contents

6   Contents

Introduction

Gary R. Collins

"IN THIS COUNTRY people walk in pairs. If you're alone, you're a misfit, an oddball, an embarrassment to your married friends who aren't quite sure how or whether to include you in their activities."

The lady who spoke these words was learning to live alone—as a widow. She might have added that single people often experience loneliness, rejection, and a feeling that they are incomplete. If you're not married somebody probably is thinking that there must be something wrong with your sex drives or your ability to get along with people. You might even be wondering about this yourself. Why aren't I married? Is there some reason why I'm not experiencing marital bliss? Am I missing God's best for my life? Is it really O.K. to be single?

The chapters in this book not only assume that it's O.K. to be single; they show that the single life can and should be rewarding and completely fulfilling. Of course there are problems. Most people *do* "walk in pairs" and those who are on their own run into frustrations because of their singleness. But married people have problems too. And the same God who created marriage never implied that the unmarried should be forced to resign themselves to a lusterless second-best kind of existence.

This book has been written by people who are experts in coping with the challenges of singleness. Most of the authors are single and several have an active involvement in working

7

with the unmarried. The chapters were prepared originally for presentation and discussion at the Continental Congress on the Family, a large interdenominational meeting conceived and directed by J. Allan Petersen, and held recently in St. Louis. Following the Congress, the authors were invited to revise their chapters for publication. The result is a collection of insightful essays, written by specialists who share a deep Christian faith and a strong desire to find practical ways for showing that it certainly is O.K. to be single.

The pages which follow cover a wide range of issues and deal both with singles who have never married and with those who were formerly married but are single now. In a stimulating and at times controversial chapter, Nancy Hardesty begins the book with a clarion call for singles to live a full and completely meaningful life style. Linda LeSourd then deals with the issues faced by single women in the church. What she has written about single women can be applied almost totally to single men, as Mark Lee's further discussion clearly demonstrates.

Virginia McIver whose own marriage collapsed leaving her with two teenagers to raise alone, Britton Wood who is minister to singles in a church attended by eight hundred unmarried adults, and Joan Campbell who faced a difficult widowhood upon the death of her husband, all write about their experiences with an insight that will be helpful to others. Robert Pinder focuses on the problems of raising children when one is a single parent without a partner to help.

Sometimes it is forgotten that teenagers and college students are also single. Their desires and concerns may differ from those of older singles, but these young people nevertheless have needs which often are not being met within the church, the home, or the society. Barbara Sroka, assistant editor of *HIS* magazine, Rich Berry who works with the Navigators on a college campus, and Denny Rydberg who edits the *Wittenburg Door* all write about the needs of the younger unmarried. The book concludes with an insightful personal essay on the Christian single life style by college president Lyle Hillegas.

Singleness is not a second-class, second-best status. It can and should be a fulfilling, satisfying way of life. The church, alerted to these issues, must become involved in a ministry to those in the congregation and community who are not married. The chapters in this book and the study guide which follows are all designed to stimulate thought and discussion among single and married readers alike. Hopefully the book will also stimulate new attitudes, new acceptance of singles and a more active church involvement with the unmarried.

GARY R. COLLINS

1.
Being Single in Today's World

Nancy Hardesty

"FOLLOW ME," Christ invites us. "Take my yoke upon you, and learn from me" (Matt. 11:29, RSV).

Mennonite theologian John Howard Yoder declares, "It needs to be taught as normative Christian truth that singleness is the first normal state for every Christian. Marriage is not wrong, and existing marriages are to be nurtured. Yet there exists no Christian imperative to become married as soon as one can or to prefer marriage over singleness as a more whole or wholesome situation." [1]

Scripture has much to teach us about developing a Christian single adult life style. Jesus' paradigm for his own relationships was not marriage but friendship. Within the Trinity he had

NANCY HARDESTY is working on a doctorate in the history of Christianity at the University of Chicago Divinity School. Previously she was assistant professor of English at Trinity College, Deerfield, Illinois. She has also been assistant editor of *Eternity* Magazine. She is co-author, with Letha Scanzoni, of *All We're Meant to Be: A Biblical Approach to Women's Liberation.*

known the most perfect of friendships. To his disciples, he said,
"You are my friends" (John 15:14, RSV). Friends for whom he
was willing to make the greatest of all sacrifices, his life. Friends
he chose. Friends with whom he shared his life and his truth.
Friends for whom he prayed. And friends whom he entreated
to "love one another" (John 15:17, RSV).

Celtic Christians of more than a millennium ago spoke of
having an *amnchara,* a "soul-friend." They had a proverb:
"Anyone without a soul-friend, an *amnchara,* is like a body
without a head." Paul Hinnebusch, in *Friendship in the Lord,*
declares: "As persons, we were made for love, we were made
for friendship and communion; for a person is complete only
in loving relationships with others." [2] It is not good for a person
to be alone, to exist in isolation, according to Genesis 2:18.
However, it is not marriage which is essential to the development
of mature personhood, but learning to live in intimacy with
another or others. Intimacy is "the need to be known," says
Hinnebusch. "Intimacy means being fully at home with someone. Home is not a place. It is where I am fully known and
loved and received just as I am. . . . Only trusted love can
give such intimacy." [3]

Jesus offered the women and men who followed him intimacy
in its fullest sense—and he expected them to offer it to each
other. "Come and see" was Jesus' invitation to Andrew (John
1:39, RSV). "We have found the Messiah," was Andrew's report to his brother Simon Peter after the visit (John 1:41, RSV).
Both became Jesus' friends forever. To the woman at the well
in Samaria, Jesus revealed himself as the Messiah who would
show her all things (John 4:25–26). And she reported to her
friends, "He told me all that I ever did" (John 4:39, RSV). He
made himself fully known to those who traveled with him. He
even took the risk of rejection: "many of his disciples went
back, and walked no more with him" (John 6:66, KJV). He
invited self-disclosure even from one as reticent as the woman

who touched only the hem of his garment (Matt. 9:20–22). In perfect love, he accepted all who came, he rejected not a one—not even the pagan woman from Syrophoenicia (Matt. 15:22–28).

"Foxes have holes, and birds of the air have nests." The Son of man had nowhere to lay his head (Matt. 8:20, RSV), yet he was perfectly at home. The psalmist declares that as "a father of the fatherless, and a judge of the widows . . . God setteth the solitary in families" (Ps. 68:5–6, KJV). Born into a nuclear family, Jesus chose instead a single adult life style in community with what sociologists today call "chosen kin." His closest friends were Peter, James and John. He was most at home in Bethany with Mary, Martha and Lazarus. When asked about his family, he replied, "Whoever does the will of my Father in heaven is my brother, and sister, and mother" (Matt. 12:50, RSV).

He was motivated in his relationships by love, not by loneliness. He knew how to be alone. He did not seek relationships to escape from coming to terms with himself. He had spent forty days alone in the wilderness, preparing himself for his mission, wrestling with all of the possible temptations to abandon it. Throughout his life he often withdrew from the crowds and even from his friends for periods of solitude and prayer. In the end he knew the aloneness of being forsaken by his friends and even by his God, yet he did not lose faith in them or in himself.

From Jesus, John learned that we are not to love "in word, neither in tongue; but in deed and in truth" (1 John 3:18, KJV). Christ was not afraid to reach out and touch others. Little children were drawn by his openness and his warmth. Mothers brought infants so "that he might touch them" (Luke 18:15, RSV). He took a child in his arms and set him in the midst of his followers to illustrate a point (Matt. 18:2). He reached out and touched one person after another, those who needed healing of the body and also of the soul. In loving humility he washed the feet of his friends, a most intimate gesture (John 13:3–17).

And he was not afraid that his gestures might be misinterpreted as seductive. He was not afraid to befriend a woman who had already had five husbands and was now living with a lover. He was not afraid to accept the loving caresses of a woman known about town as a "sinner" (Luke 7:37). Others questioned his integrity because he accepted her attention, but he knew she touched him in love, not lust. Fully at home with his own sexuality, totally aware and yet in control of his own sexual feelings, he could enjoy the loving touch of Mary of Bethany as she washed his weary feet, massaged them with a fragrant ointment, and dried them with her flowing hair (John 12:1–3). Nor was he hesitant to hold John to his breast as they reclined at the last supper (John 13:23–25).

"Having loved his own who were in the world," John says, "he loved them to the end" (John 13:1, RSV). John, Peter and Paul all repeat his words: "Love one another." The Epistle to Diognetus reports concerning the early Christians, "They love everyone."

Paul did say "it is better to marry than to be aflame with passion" (1 Cor. 7:9, RSV). But he clearly preferred the single life and advised others that they would be better off to adopt it (1 Cor. 7:7, 8, 11, 26, 27, 28, 32, 34, 38, 40). As Yoder concludes, Paul's position, like that of Jesus, was clearly "marriage is fine but singleness is better." [4] Paul too knew what it meant to be alone, but he did not lead a lonely life. "Do we not have the right to be accompanied by a wife?" Paul once asked rhetorically (1 Cor. 9:5, RSV). Of course he had that right. But instead he chose to fill his life with a variety of friends. He traveled with Barnabas, who was probably older than himself; with Timothy ("my beloved child," 2 Tim. 1:2, RSV) and John Mark, who were younger; with Luke, the physician, who could attend to his illness. He lived for periods of time with

Lydia and with Priscilla and Aquila. He often concluded his letters with phrases like "My love be with you all" (1 Cor. 16:24, RSV) and words of warmest commendation for male friends such as Tychicus ("the beloved brother," Eph. 6:21, RSV), Onesimus ("the faithful and beloved brother," Col. 4:9, RSV), Luke and Demas; and for female friends such as Phoebe ("for she has been a ruler of many and of myself also," Rom. 16:2, Bushnell [5]), Junia, Tryphaena and Tryphosa, Julia (Rom. 16: 7, 12, 15, KJV), Euodia and Syntyche ("for they have labored side by side with me in the gospel," Phil. 4:3, RSV), the household of Nympha (Col. 4:15). Paul implied that he chose a single adult life style and recommended it for others because he found it most conducive to his primary calling to serve God. "I want you to be free from anxieties," was how he put it (1 Cor. 7:32 ff., RSV). Married persons must in good conscience be primarily concerned with the welfare of their spouses and their children. Their interests are divided. Unmarried persons are free to be primarily concerned about the affairs of the Lord, serving God and serving others in God's name.

Many Christians throughout the ages have shared Paul's viewpoint. Jerome extolled the joys and virtues of the celibate life for virgins and those whose spouses had died. He even went so far as to say that he saw no reason for Christians to have children of their own—pagans would produce sufficient offspring as raw material for spiritual rebirth! The monastic life provided opportunities for solitary prayer and devotion, a community in which to find mutual support and avenues of service to others. Church history is studded with stories of single people whose service to God was nourished by communal religious life and by the deepest of friendships: Augustine and his community of monks; Jerome and Paula; Basil, Gregory of Nyssa and Gregory of Nazianzus; Catherine of Siena and Raymond of Capua, Teresa of Avila and John of the Cross; Bernard of Clairvaux and William of Thierry. Their biographies and letters give us a wealth of insights into living a Christian adult single life. They believed as Aelred of Rievaulx says in *De Spirituali Amicitia,* "There can be no genuine happiness without a friend." [6]

One of the most unfortunate consequences of the Protestant Reformation was the disavowal of monastic life, the dissolution of religious communities in most Protestant churches. Seeing only the abuses of the monastic system and not its virtues they abolished it rather than trying to reform it. Many Protestants have forgotten the Pauline ideal so totally and have isolated themselves so completely from the riches of spiritual life still maintained in the Catholic tradition that one can find ridiculous statements like the following in a book often recommended for teens: "The plan of the Creator is marriage, not singleness. . . . The plan of God is marriage. Singleness for religious service is a cultural tradition and not the plan of God." [7] In actual fact, singleness has rarely, if ever, been a "cultural tradition"—most cultures strongly encourage marriage in order to perpetuate their own existence. An authentic choice between singleness and marriage is indeed one important ramification of the Christian gospel's emphasis on the kingdom of God rather than the kingdoms of earth, on spiritual rebirth rather than on physical parenthood. The formation of the Christian church, the family of God, offered people the option of moving beyond the family and tribe of blood-kin into the wider community of faith. As Paul says, "Having gifts that differ according to the grace given to us, let us use them" (Rom. 12:6, RSV).

Despite his warning against conforming to the norms of this world, we as Protestant Christians today have generally accepted the world's misconceptions. We have equated intimacy with sexual intercourse; we have decided that lack of sexual relations is contrary to "nature"; and thus we have concluded that marriage is essential to full personhood. We give our young people booklets such as *How to Get a Husband for Christian Girls* which informs them that "it's the abnormal girl who doesn't want marriage" and that "it's the natural thing for girls to find their highest usefulness in the joys and accomplishments of a happy home." Without a shred of scriptural evidence, we encourage them to believe that within God's "wise, detailed, complete" plan for their lives "is to be found the Mr. Prince Charming Husband who . . . has been selected with all the omniscience of God . . . . planned to perfectly fit your need." All they must do is "want it earnestly, [with] every fiber of your being. . . . want it more than you want anything else in life." [8] Did not Jesus say rather that it is God whom we are to love with every fiber of our being and our neighbor (not our spouse) whom we are to love as ourselves?

According to the 1970 census figures, nearly 7 million Americans, both men and women, past the age of thirty have not as yet married; 11 million have been widowed and 4.5 million have been divorced. Yet they all have essentially the same needs and struggles as do those who are married. All persons must find their own individual identity, must come to terms with themselves in their aloneness. They search for security, a place to belong, a home, a "family" in which to live. They reach out for intimacy, for closeness, touch, union with another. They strive for achievement, a sense of accomplishment, of mission, to give life meaning.

The Body of Christ must include a variety of life styles. We dare not absolutize one as normative, or we run the risk of saying to a vital arm or eye, "We have no need of you." And if the church is to include single as well as married people, we must continue to grapple with certain biblical issues:

• As Christians we find our identity in the fact that in Christ we are new creations (2 Cor. 5:17). Our identity is not based on nationality, race, sex, economic class or marital status.

• We believe, as Dietrich Bonhoeffer says, that "through the call of Jesus [people] become individuals. Willy-nilly, they are compelled to decide, and that decision can only be made by themselves. It is no choice of their own that makes them individuals; it is Christ who makes them individuals by calling

them. Every [person] is called separately, and must follow
alone." [9]

• As Christians, our sense of security is to be found in our
faith in God, not in any temporal, cultural social institution.

• Our home is the church, our family the body of believers.
No definition of "family" can be called Christian which does
not include single people, religious communities, tribes, even
polygamous households, in addition to the twentieth-century,
post-Victorian, suburban American nuclear family.

• Our definitions of intimacy must begin with friendship, not
marriage, as their paradigm. Christ calls all Christians to friendship, but not all to marriage.

• Our thinking about closeness and touch should be concrete,
contemporary embodiments of such biblical injunctions as
"greet one another with a holy kiss" (Rom. 16:16, RSV), "lay
hands on the sick" (Mark 16:18, KJV), "wash one another's
feet" (John 13:14, RSV), and "love one another" (John 15:17,
RSV).

• Our theology of sexuality must be based on a model of
personhood rather than of marriage; it must apply as fully to
the single person as to the married. Our ethical thinking about
such topics as masturbation, love play, intercourse, fornication,
adultery and homosexuality must include the single adult in
addition to adolescents, engaged couples and married persons.

• Our definition of achievement, especially for women, must
be broader than parenthood. We must recover a sense of vocation, a sense of using *all* our gifts and talents to the glory of
God.

• Our sense of mission, our service to God, must take prior-
ity over all other areas of life.

Peter once asked Jesus, " 'We have left everything to follow
you! What then will there be for us?' " (Matt. 19:27, NIV).
Jesus assured him, " 'I tell you the truth, . . . no one who has
left home or wife or brothers or parents or children for the sake
of the kingdom of God will fail to receive many times as much

in this age and, in the age to come, eternal life.' " (Luke 18: 29–30, NIV).

In *The Cost of Discipleship,* Dietrich Bonhoeffer comments on this passage: "Though we all have to enter upon discipleship alone, we do not remain alone. If we take him [Jesus] at his word and dare to become individuals, our reward is the fellowship of the Church. Here is a visible brotherhood [and sisterhood] to compensate a hundredfold for all we have lost." [10] In Bonhoeffer's own life, discipleship involved the renunciation of marriage. But he was rewarded by the fellowship of the Confessing Church, the love of the community of seminarians for whom he wrote *Life Together,* and the friendship of Eberhard Bethge.

Ida Scudder said no to a proposal of marriage from a man she came to love during her medical school years in the United States. Instead she answered the call of God to practice medicine among the women of India. During her nearly sixty years of service there at Vellore, she built hospitals, a school of nursing and a medical college. She was surrounded by the love of staff, students and patients. For thirty years she was supported by the devoted friendship of Gertrude Dodd, who gave up her own life in New York City to embody the words of Ruth to Naomi, "Wherever you go, I will go; wherever you live, I will live. Your people will be my people, and your God will be my God" (Ruth 1:16, TEV).

Others sometimes think of single people as deprived of a precious part of life. We sometimes think of ourselves as lacking something, but James says: "You do not have, because you do not ask" (James 4:2, RSV). God stands ready always to "fulfill all your needs, in Christ Jesus, as lavishly as only God can" (Phil. 4:19, JB)!

Notes

1. John H. Yoder, *Singleness in Ethical and Pastoral Perspective* (Elkhart, Ind.: Associated Mennonite Biblical Seminaries, 1974), pp. 3–4.

2. Paul Hinnebusch, *Friendship in the Lord* (Notre Dame, Ind.: Ave Maria Press, 1974), p. 34.

3. Ibid., p. 35.

4. Yoder, *Singleness,* p. 10.

5. Katharine C. Bushnell, *God's Word to Women* (Oakland, Calif.: privately printed by the author, 1930), para. 367.

6. Donald Goergen, *The Sexual Celibate* (New York: The Seabury Press, 1974), p. 167.

7. Herbert J. Miles, *Sexual Understanding Before Marriage* (Grand Rapids, Mich.: Zondervan Publishing House, 1971), p. 177.

8. William W. Orr, *How to Get a Husband for Christian Girls* (Wheaton, Ill.: Van Kampen Press, n.d.), pp. 2, 32.

9. Dietrich Bonhoeffer, *The Cost of Discipleship* (New York: The Macmillan Company, 1959), p. 105.

10. Ibid., p. 113.

For Additional Reading

Bonhoeffer, Dietrich. *Life Together*. New York: Harper & Row, Publishers, 1954.

Evening, Margaret. *Who Walk Alone*. Downers Grove, Ill.: Inter-Varsity Press, 1974.

Greeley, Andrew. *The Friendship Game*. Garden City, N.Y.: Doubleday and Company, 1970.

Maslow, Abraham. *Motivation and Personality*. New York: Harper & Row, 1970.

Payne, Dorothy. *Women Without Men*. Philadelphia: Pilgrim Press, 1969.

Ryan, John and Mary. *Love and Sexuality: A Christian Approach*. New York: Holt, Rinehart and Winston, 1967.

Scanzoni, Letha. *Sex Is a Parent Affair*. Glendale, Calif.: Regal Books, 1973.

Scanzoni, Letha and Nancy Hardesty. *All We're Meant to Be.* Waco, Texas: Word Books, 1974.

Thurian, Max. *Marriage and Celibacy.* London: SCM Press, 1969.

2.
Living Creatively: The Single Woman and the Church

Linda LeSourd

THE SINGLE Christian woman is in a peculiar position today. She battles insecurity, loneliness and frustration in a unique way. In many cases she has no sense of roots; she is most often independent of her family and does not consider their home to be hers. She does not experience the fulfillment of a life-building relationship with a man, and cannot thus share her *total* self—emotionally, sexually, intellectually and spiritually— with another, cannot bear and raise her own children. Furthermore, in evangelical circles she is often frustrated in her attempts to use her gifts in ministry or leadership.

What does the Bible have to say to the single woman? With the exception of the widowed, very little is directed toward the particulars of her situation. When the Scriptures were written, her problems did not exist as we know them now. In New

LINDA LESOURD works with Cornerstone, a discipleship and training center for college students and young adults in the Washington, D.C., and College Park, Md., area. Her duties involve administration as well as training. She is a graduate of Ohio Wesleyan University.

Testament times, single women remained under the roof and authority of their families until they were married. Actually, it was a disgrace for a woman to be single. Widows provide the exception, although it was only the New Testament writings and the practices of the early church which lifted widows into a position of respect and honor.[1]

The New Testament writers exhorted the believers to care for the widows, and provided these women with an avenue of ministry.[2] It is my contention that today's church should, in like fashion, concern itself with *all* single women—widowed, divorced or never married—taking special care to minister to their unique needs and allowing them to contribute their gifts freely and responsibly to the upbuilding of the whole Body of Christ.

The needs of the single woman vary widely. In this country alone 16.5 million women over twenty-five are single. That includes never married, widowed, and divorced women who range across the whole spectrum economically, socially, intellectually.[3] Though generalizations are unfair, they are inescapable in a discussion of this nature. Therefore, it must be remembered that the following directives must be personalized and modified to fit particular women and localized bodies of believers. This chapter primarily addresses the situation of young, never-married single women. However, much of what is said will also apply to those who are older, widowed or divorced.

Before beginning, two definitions are needed. First, when speaking to "the church," I will be referring primarily to the institutional church. In essence, however, the church consists of no more and no less than those who believe in and follow Jesus Christ as their Lord and Savior.

Since I am addressing the church's ministry to single women and their ministry within the church, it is also necessary to define *ministry*. Preaching and teaching the assembled body is not enough. Ministry must be personalized to the needs of the individual, that each one might grow to completeness in Christ (Col. 1:25–28). Paul urges the early Christians to "teach and admonish one another" (Col. 3:16, RSV). All must participate in ministry, for all are ministers of the gospel (2 Cor. 5:18–20). Leaders are given to the Body of Christ *to equip each individual to minister* (Eph. 4:12, RSV, 2nd ed.); the body grows as each member is fully contributing his or her part (Eph. 4:16).

Even more important, we must remember that to minister means *to serve*. Jesus gave us the pattern: "For even the Son of Man did not come to be served, but to serve, and to give His life a ransom for many" (Mark 10:45, NAS).

The Church's Ministry to the Single Woman

Ministry should be directed at meeting genuine needs. William Glasser says that the basic human needs are for a feeling of self-worth and to give and receive love in the context of responsible relationships.[4] Christians have another need: to grow into maturity in Christ. Let us examine these needs as they relate to single women and suggest ways the church can effectively address itself to meeting them.

Adjusting to not being married is perhaps the most common problem of single Christian women. Most want to marry, and some feel inadequate, rejected or even guilty because they have not. Our culture strongly encourages the woman to find her identity in relation to a man, and the Bible tells her that she has actually been created for him (Gen. 2:18–24; 1 Cor. 11:9). The dilemma for the Christian is more painful than for the non-Christian. Not only is she, like the unbeliever, culturally conditioned from birth that fulfillment for a woman is only in marriage, but the church lifts and heralds marriage as the highest, noblest life style.

On the other hand, the New Testament actually exalts singleness as a state of high calling. Jesus spoke of singleness as a gift (Matt. 19:10–12), and Paul asserted that it was a blessing to be single (1 Cor. 7:8, 26, 28). The Word of God tells us that each of us is complete in Christ (Col. 2:10, KJV). *Complete* means "lacking in nothing . . . full . . . whole . . . inclusion of all that is needed for perfection or fulfillment." Thus it is possible to lead a fulfilled life without marriage. A woman's identity and sense of self-worth can be found in Christ alone and should not depend upon a husband. Single women need to be taught that marriage, like singleness, is primarily a calling from God (1 Cor. 7:17). It must be remembered that Paul considered the responsibilities and difficulties of marriage to be so great that he recommended the single life to the Corinthians (1 Cor. 7:8, 28, 32–35).

Most younger single women, however, will at some point marry, as will a number of older singles. The single woman should realize that it is not wrong to desire marriage or to prepare herself for it, but she will waste valuable years if she builds her life upon the hope or prospect of a marriage which may never come.

Singles should be encouraged to build today the values and life styles they want in the future. Too few realize that they need not be married to enjoy a home or share life with another person. In fact, investing time and creativity in making a present house or apartment a home helps establish for them a much-needed sense of security and identity apart from marriage. Living with others and having to share meals, responsibilities and possessions forces their personal and spiritual growth.

As the church teaches that marriage is living in partnership, it needs to encourage single women to live in partnership with others *now*. As it teaches that marriage involves submission to one another, it must help single women learn to submit to others *now*. Many single women refuse to work out small conflicts with roommates, co-workers or friends, not realizing that they are building destructive life patterns which in time will lead to loneliness and frustration, perhaps even isolation.

When a woman realizes that her need for love, security and deep relationships with others can be effectively met outside

of marriage, she is far more likely to adjust creatively to singleness. One of the best ways to have such needs met is to be
actively involved in a close, caring community of believers. This
is what the church should be. Consider the New Testament
church community:

> They were continually devoting themselves to the apostles' teach-
> ing and to fellowship, to the breaking of bread and to prayer.
> . . . And all those who had believed were together, and had
> all things in common; and they began selling their property and
> possessions, and were sharing them with all, as anyone might have
> need. And day by day continuing with one mind in the temple,
> and breaking bread from house to house, they were taking their
> meals together. . . .
> . . . not one of them claimed that anything belonging to him
> was his own; but all things were common property. . . . there
> was not a needy person among them . . . (Acts 2:42, 44–46;
> 4:32, 34, NAS).

Unfortunately, few modern church fellowships exemplify
this kind of dedication and commitment. As a result, Christians
hungering for a shared life with other believers are often dissatisfied with the church. This is especially true for singles lacking the fullness of a family life. Few of them realize how far
such a caring community would go toward meeting deep needs
they have previously associated with marriage.

Today men and women of all ages and backgrounds are
drawing together into communities of all types and sizes.[5]
Building a stable community takes years, and most churches do
not feel called to pursue such a task. Yet there are many aspects of genuine Christian community which can be incorporated into the local church right now. Diversity, commitment,
love and deep relationships are four such characteristics which
are especially important to the single woman. Let us examine
these as they relate to the church.

In metropolitan areas where singles cluster, active churches usually provide a group especially for them. Meetings and social events with other singles alleviate the potential loneliness and isolation of not being married. Many of these groups provide a valuable ministry, especially attracting non-Christians who frequently come to Christ as a result. Some truly are a caring fellowship of Christians encouraging each other to grow as individuals in Christ.[6] Yet such groups suffer from inherent instability; upon marrying, members "graduate" to a young marrieds' group, indicating that involvement in either is primarily based on one's marital state. Single groups are usually heavily conditioned toward marriage, and thus perpetuate the myth that marriage is the ultimate solution to all one's problems. Frequently, they are characterized by a heavy dating emphasis which fosters game-playing and superficiality in relationships, especially between men and women. Such problems eventually undermine the spiritual quality of the fellowship. At times, the church leadership seems insensitive to these dynamics and neglects to provide the spiritual guidance and redirection needed by the group.

As an alternative, some churches provide young adult groups, incorporating both singles and marrieds. Better still, singles should be involved in the total church community where they can enjoy the diversity of the whole Body of Christ.

Singles especially need close involvement with families. There they can observe firsthand the needs, struggles and loneliness experienced by those who are married in order to gain a more realistic picture of marriage. This lays the groundwork for building better marriages in the future, should they marry, and often gives them a new appreciation of the advantages of being single. On the other hand, singles need models of happy, fulfilled marriage relationships, for many are apprehensive about marriage and need to see that with Christ at the center it can and does work. Families within the church can be encouraged to involve singles in their family activities. Children, married couples and the aged provide needed balance and fresh perspectives for the single. Likewise, the insights and energies of the single person contribute greatly to the lives of others in the church.

The Bible calls Christians to care for each other's physical needs (James 2:14–18). As we see in Acts, upon conversion the first Christians instinctively began to share all they had, indicating a willingness to commit themselves without reserve to each other. Today's Christians talk a great deal about love, but without commitment borne out in action, such words are meaningless. "Let us not love with word or with tongue, but in deed and truth" (1 John 3:18, NAS).

The single woman often lacks a sense of security, which can be provided by having a group of people committed to caring for her needs and sharing in the totality of her life. This might translate into friends who give their time to help with undertakings like moving or house painting, who lend advice in the purchase or repair of a car, or who assist with a sudden financial need. A single woman may desire counsel or assistance on practical things such as insurance, finances, household repairs, medical or legal affairs. If laypersons within the church community will make themselves available to help with such matters, the church can serve as a clearinghouse. Churches usually have access to a wealth of practical information and can provide a valuable ministry by linking people up with those who can meet their needs. This is all part of what Paul meant when he said, "Bear one another's burdens, and thus fulfil the law of Christ" (Gal. 6:2, NAS).

I spoke earlier of the woman's need to love and be loved. A good church fellowship often seems very warm and loving to the single at first. Yet for her need for love to be adequately met, she needs a handful of others who know and truly love her as an individual. Brothers and sisters who can be counted on to rejoice in her victories and stand by her in failure or grief are perhaps a single woman's greatest treasure. She needs friends who will pray her through crises and help her sort out her feelings, fears and goals. True friends will speak the truth in love with her and encourage her to do likewise (Eph. 4:15). That not only entails giving genuine affection and affirmation whenever possible, but also Spirit-led correction when it is needed.

Many single women idealistically expect that they will be fulfilled overnight in a marriage relationship, able to share their deepest thoughts, able to love and be loved unselfishly, although they have never yet even approached such depth with another person. The single needs to cultivate deep relationships with both men and women right now. (I have noted that the woman who has a number of very close male friends is usually less frustrated with being single than the one who does not.) If she eventually marries, building those relationships will serve as good preparation. If not, having intimate friendships with both sexes will go far to prevent loneliness.

In *Life Together,* Dietrich Bonhoeffer shows that we can be in the midst of Christian fellowship and experience the worst kind of loneliness:

> He who is alone with his sin is utterly alone. It may be that Christians, notwithstanding corporate worship, common prayer, and all their fellowship in service, may still be left to their loneliness. The final breakthrough to fellowship does not occur, because, though they have fellowship with one another as believers and as devout people, they do not have fellowship as the undevout, as sinners. The pious fellowship permits no one to be a sinner. So everybody must conceal his sin from himself and from the fellowship. We dare not be sinners. Many Christians are unthinkably horrified when a real sinner is suddenly discovered among the righteous. So we remain alone with our sin, living in lies and hypocrisy.[7]

Bonhoeffer goes on to point out the necessity of confessing our sins to each other. Paul Tournier, Bruce Larson and others emphasize the need for vulnerability in relationships.[8] Yet our

culture heralds independence, lauds those who are successful and
can make it on their own. Because we *are* all sinners, this encourages hypocrisy and serves to insulate individuals from
exposing their real needs and having them effectively met. The
single woman especially falls prey to this. To ward off pity or
judgment for not being married, she may try to appear strong,
peaceful and victorious, though inside she is crumbling. Of even
greater concern is the single woman who actually believes herself to be self-sufficient. If she defensively hardens herself
against showing her weaknesses or need for others, she only
hurts her chances of ever marrying or of adjusting successfully
to sharing life with a man, should she marry. She may dis-
qualify herself from the kind of authentic relationships which
can be built only by those who are willing to be vulnerable and
share their weaknesses with each other. The most secure love
a single woman can experience is from those who, knowing her
failings and darkest sins, continue to love, forgive and accept
her.

There is a danger of the Christian fellowship becoming so
sanctimonious that those with deep unresolved problems are
frightened into silence or hypocrisy. This is especially true in
the area of sex. Some singles find it very difficult to handle the
lack of sexual fulfillment; others suffer aftereffects of our
warped cultural attitudes toward sex; still others are badly mis-
informed with regard to sexual matters; and many are heavily
burdened with feelings of guilt. A significant number of seemingly innocent Christian women wrestle with problems of
homosexuality, immorality, rape and sexual molestation. The
church has a responsibility to minister forgiveness, new life and
healing to such women. Only as such problems and anxieties
are brought out into the open and resolved through sensitive
counseling and good teaching from a biblical perspective will
the single woman grow as a whole person.

Finally, ministering to the single woman means helping her

grow as a disciple of Jesus Christ. One of the most effective ways of accomplishing this is for a more stable and mature believer to spend time with her in one-to-one discipleship training. As Jesus took the disciples with him, and they participated communally in the daily activities of life, likewise a discipling relationship works best when those involved enjoy times of working, eating, traveling and relaxing together, as well as times of prayer and study. Parachurch ministries like the Navigators and others can teach the church much in this regard. Such relationships cannot be programed, but they can be encouraged, especially by having trained men and women available for those singles who are interested in pursuing their spiritual growth in this manner. Although it is usually more natural for women to work with other women, this should not prohibit men from also playing a part in the discipleship of women. Paul provides the model for this kind of ministry in his relationship with the Thessalonians: "Having thus a fond affection for you, we were well pleased to impart to you not only the gospel but also our own lives, because you had become very dear to us" (1 Thess. 2:8, NAS).

Jesus personally discipled at least twelve men. However, no one of us can effectively disciple even one other person on our own; we are corporately the Body of Christ, and we need the gifts and input of each other. A Christian community or small group meeting regularly within the church can provide an excellent atmosphere for growth in discipleship for the single woman. She needs a place to share her weaknesses and struggles and receive counsel and strength. With their tendency toward isolation, singles need to be educated as to how such an intimate fellowship can aid their spiritual growth. Discovering this, some then find it helpful for the group to hold them accountable in certain areas of their lives.

Single women sometimes express the regret that they are not exhorted and challenged to spiritual greatness. The church has a responsibility to take the gifts and ministries of single women seriously, for they are given by Christ for the benefit of all believers. Thus single women need to be equipped as full contributors to the upbuilding of the Body of Christ.

The Ministry of the Single Woman

The primary purpose of singleness, according to Paul, is "to secure undistracted devotion to the Lord" (1 Cor. 7:35, NAS). The single woman has time and freedom to give herself to the things of the Lord in a way a married woman cannot (1 Cor. 7:34). As a member of the Body of Christ, she has been equipped with natural talents and with gifts of the Holy Spirit; as a single woman she is held back only by ignorance of her call to minister or unwillingness to follow it. Because any encounter with another person can provide an opportunity to minister, every Christian woman can be involved in the Lord's work full time, even if she never chooses it as a vocation.

Guidelines for a single woman's ministry within the church are difficult to establish. There are two schools of thought in evangelical circles today, as briefly sketched below. Both sides base their stands on Scripture, and both raise issues which cannot easily be refuted. Rather than choosing one or the other, I suggest that women need to hear and apply *both* views to their personal lives and corporate ministries; unfortunately most women opt for one at the expense of the other. We must guard against allowing cultural or personal biases to color our interpretation of the Bible.

First, there is a call among concerned Christians for the elimination of any restrictions within the church on the basis of sex; they assert that women should be able to exercise all the gifts and ministries, including being ordained as pastors and advancing to the very top leadership positions. There is a good scriptural case for this view. To begin with, Jesus revolutionized the role of women. Going directly against the social mores of his day, he talked with women, allowed them to travel with him (Luke 8:2–3), healed them, defended their rights in marriage (Mark 10:2–12), allowed even the most despised of them to touch him publicly (Luke 7:36–50; Mark 5:24–34), and loved and respected them as some of his closest friends. In thus treating them as persons, as equals, as friends, he restored to women the equal value before God given them at creation.

Furthermore, the Holy Spirit filled, empowered and gave gifts to men and women alike at Pentecost and continues to do so today. In the New Testament, women were prophetesses (Acts 21:9; 1 Cor. 11:5), teachers (Acts 18:26; Titus 2:3), and deaconesses (Rom. 16:1). Paul's first convert in Europe was an influential woman (Acts 16:13–15); she and others had churches meeting in their homes (see Col. 4:14). Before God, men and women are equally responsible to minister as evidenced by Paul's referring to women as "fellow workers" (Rom. 16:3; Phil. 4:3, RSV), and Peter's calling them "fellow-heirs of the grace of life" (1 Pet. 3:7, NAS). Moreover, Paul states that "in the Lord, neither is woman independent of man, nor is man independent of woman" (1 Cor. 11:11, NAS), and that "there is neither male nor female; for you are all one in Christ Jesus" (Gal. 3:28, RSV).

In an article entitled, "Jesus, Women and the Resurrection," Virginia Mollenkott uses the fact that women were the first witnesses of the resurrection to argue for taking women more seriously in the church. She asserts that Jesus was not offended when Mary Magdalene was aggressive and self-assertive; rather it was at that point he commissioned her with proclaiming to the disciples the important message of his resurrection (John 20:15–17). The author concludes with this exhortation to women:

When Jesus tells a modern Mary that she is to go unto His brethren and speak to them, she had better go and speak to them; and when she speaks, Christ's brethren had better listen.[9]

For a very thorough and well-documented argument for full participation of women in all aspects of ministry, I suggest Letha Scanzoni and Nancy Hardesty's book, *All We're Meant to Be.*[10]

Ultimately, each single woman must earnestly seek to find and follow Christ's unique calling in her life; she is responsible before God not only to discern what ministry he has for her but to prepare herself to carry it out. The challenge to utilize their potential more fully for kingdom work is desperately needed for those who regard themselves as unimportant and prefer to defer to men or to more aggressive women. They need to be shown that by not fully using the gifts given them by God, they are actually robbing the Body of Christ of some of its strength and resources.

On the other hand, many Christians believe that women should have a supportive role in ministry, remaining under the leadership and final authority of men. Scriptural evidences for this include the creation of woman from the rib of Adam for the purpose of being a helper to him (Gen. 2:18, 22–23; 1 Cor. 11:9) and the headship of man over woman (Gen. 3:16; 1 Cor. 11:3). Women are prohibited from speaking in church (1 Cor. 14:34–35), and from teaching or exercising authority over a man (1 Tim. 2:12). All of this is not to mention the passages instructing wives to submit to their husbands (Eph. 5:22–23; Col. 3:18; 1 Pet. 3:1–6), which do not directly concern single women but nonetheless imply the general leadership of men over women.

Rather than dismissing this view as cultural in origin, let us examine its merits and see what it has to say to a modern single woman in the church. The concept of submission goes directly against our natural tendencies toward independence, aggressiveness and self-assertiveness—all heralded as virtues in today's culture. Much of the debate on the submission of women revolves around the question of authority; the world says you need to be "in charge" to be important, that leadership is the highest calling. Traditionally assigned the unglamorous jobs and restrained from authority and leadership in the church, women today are understandably anxious to improve their position.

Christ indeed has set women free from all manner of bondage, and their gifts and ministries should not be suppressed. Jesus commended stewardship of gifts as good and important (Matt. 25:21), but he said that the only way to be *great* is to be a servant:

> You know that those who are recognized as rulers of the Gentiles lord it over them; and their great men exercise authority over them. But it is not so among you, but whoever wishes to become great among you shall be your servant; and whoever wishes to be first among you shall be slave of all. For even the Son of Man did not come to be served, but to serve, and to give His life as a ransom for many (Mark 10:42–45, NAS).

Thus Christ reverses our concept of leadership, calling us to lay down our lives for one another. Likewise the apostles remind us that our freedom and gifts are given only so that we may better serve others:

> . . . do not turn your freedom into an opportunity for the flesh, but through love serve one another (Gal. 5:13, NAS).

> As each one has received a special gift, employ it in serving one another, as good stewards of the manifold grace of God. . . . clothe yourselves with humility toward one another, for God is opposed to the proud, but gives grace to the humble (1 Pet. 4:10; 5:5, NAS).

Both men and women are called to service and to submission (Eph. 5:21), and submission is underlined for women in the Bible (1 Tim. 2:11; 1 Pet. 3:1–6; 1 Cor. 14:34). To many, submission connotes weakness or inferiority. Yet this is not the scriptural perspective. Jesus was equal and one with God the Father, the Creator of the universe. He chose to give up his power, rights and authority temporarily, submitted himself in obedience to the Father and devoted his life to serving and ministering to others. When they are certain of who they are before God, women need not fear submitting themselves to him and to fellow believers. In fact, the key to Jesus' being able to humble himself and be a servant is found in his total security in who he was and in his calling from God (John 13:3). In practicing this attitude of service and submission to others, however, there is a danger of using it as a technique to control others through subtle manipulation. Serving cannot be a means to achieve power or greatness. It is the end in itself.

Francis Schaeffer emphasizes the importance of taking the lowest place until God *forces* us into a position of leadership in a sermon entitled, "No Little People, No Little Places." [11] As a safeguard, a single Christian woman is wise to refrain from launching out in a leadership ministry except as she is commissioned and supported by a body of believers. Moreover, it is my conviction that a close committed fellowship is needed to provide insight and encouragement for the single woman as she seeks to determine her gifts and calling. To confirm God's leading in her life, a stable group of brothers and sisters who know her well should be involved in her decision making. Since spiritual gifts are given for the common good (1 Cor. 12:7; Eph. 4:12), she is accountable to the body as to how they are used. One important criterion for her to consider in assessing her calling is the needs of those with whom she works and their ability to receive what she has to offer. The body can help her with this and serve as a "home base" where she is nurtured and recharged spiritually. This is especially important for the woman who is surrounded daily by the values and pressures of the world in her job or for one who is looked up to as a leader or counselor.

There are countless types of ministry available to the single woman today, and we can find scriptural precedents for women involved in a wide variety of ministries. In the Old Testament the skilled women made use of their training and ability in the building of the tabernacle (Exod. 35:25–26). Today the natural talents and creative energies of women involved in the arts, business, medicine, counseling and other fields can be dynamically utilized within the church. We are instructed to show hospitality to strangers and to fellow believers (Heb. 13:2; Rom. 12:13), which can open the door to a powerful ministry. The enthusiasm of Lydia serves as a good example—she "urged" and "prevailed upon" the apostles to stay with her (Acts 16:15, NAS). Let us not underestimate the importance of having a ministry through contributing financially to the work of others. The women who contributed to the ministry of Jesus and the disciples apparently were involved in other ways as well (Luke 8:1–3).

As the Samaritan woman ran and told her city about her encounter with Jesus, women today should be involved in evangelism (John 4:39). As Philip's daughters prophesied (Acts 21:9), so women today can speak God's Word, in all wisdom and discernment, to his people. The ministry of women to men is open to debate, primarily because of one verse in 1 Timothy prohibiting women to "teach or exercise authority over a man" (2:12). Yet there is no question that women are needed to minister to other women, especially in small groups or one-to-one discipling relationships. The love and commitment between Ruth and Naomi can serve as a model for the kind of relationships we need to cultivate today.

Working as a team with other men and women is an exciting way to minister. Scriptural protoypes of this include Priscilla's teaching ministry with her husband (Acts 18:26) and Euodia and Syntyche, who are referred to as Paul's fellow workers (Phil. 4:2–3). The power of two or more teaching, counseling and sharing together in this way far outdistances that of one alone. (See Matt. 18:19–20; Eccles. 4:9–12; John 13:35; 17:21, 23.) Not only does the diversity of gifts and insights multiply the impact, but any message is beautifully validated when love and commitment are evident among those who are ministering.

The Great Commandment is to love God above all else. Ministering to others often diverts the Christian from this purpose, and single women need to heed the example of Mary's undistracted devotion to her Lord and to his Word (John 12:3; Luke 10:39, 42). The ministry of prayer is of great importance, for the New Testament abounds with promises that God will act in accordance with the prayers of his people (John 14:12–14; 15:7; Matt. 7:7–11). Widows in the early church ministered primarily through prayer and by caring for the sick and needy (1 Tim. 5:5, 10).[12] It is said of Dorcas that she was "abounding with deeds of kindness and charity" (Acts 9:36, NAS). This exemplifies a ministry single women—together with all other Christians—are called to perform: caring for the afflicted, the lonely, the imprisoned; feeding the hungry; visiting the orphans and widows (Jer. 22:15–16; Matt. 25:34–40; James 1:27).

I have spent much time pointing out the responsibilities of the church to the single woman. The church does indeed need to take steps to help her establish a sense of self-worth, to provide a loving, caring community and to equip her as a disciple of Christ. It has been said that people stop believing in religion when it does not meet their needs. The church today is in danger of losing the involvement of the single woman because its family emphasis, program orientation and separation of singles leaves her needs unmet. It is often the parachurch ministries or groups of Christians assembling outside the institutional church which more effectively serve as the ministering body of believers the church should be, especially for the unmarried. If the institutional church is to meet the needs of its members and fulfill its calling in the world, it must seek to learn from such groups and work in partnership with them.

On the other hand, there is a grave danger if the attitude of the single woman is one of demanding that her needs be met by the church or any body of believers. She must first remember that ultimately it is only God himself who can supply all of her needs. Secondly, though she has a great need to be loved and cared for, her greater need is to lose her life for others and the sake of the gospel if she is to be fulfilled (Matt. 16:25; 19:29). Since she has no spouse and usually no children to demand her self-sacrificing love, the single woman is more prone to selfishness than one who is married. Thus the single woman needs a vision and sense of mission to which she can commit herself—a calling which will maximize her gifts and make the most of the freedom and time uniquely available to her.

The institutional church may not attract her, but she must not let its failures keep her away. God promises to meet our needs, and for her that may be outside the church; yet she is to go to the church to serve. Let the single woman commit herself to the church, not for her own comfort and satisfaction, but because the church best represents the totality and richness of the whole Body of Christ. She is to commit herself to that body because it is designed as a "context in which God is creating a new people in the midst of a fallen and broken world." [13]

Notes

1. Charles Caldwell Ryrie, *The Role of Women in the Church* (Chicago: Moody Press, 1970 [formerly published as *The Place of Women in the Church,* 1958]), pp. 65, 139–40.

2. Acts 6:1; 1 Tim. 5:3–16; James 1:27. Ryrie, *The Role of Women in the Church,* pp. 81–85, 139–40.

3. Figures are taken from the *Statistical Abstract of the United States, 1974,* p. 48.

4. William Glasser, *Reality Therapy* (New York: Harper & Row, 1965), pp. 8–10.

5. Suggested reading on community includes anything by Elizabeth O'Connor or Gordon Cosby on The Church of The Saviour in Washington, D.C., and *Living Together in a World Falling Apart* by Dave and Neta Jackson (Carol Stream, Illinois: Creation House, 1974).

6. *Guideposts* magazine recently cited South Main Baptist Church in Houston, Texas, for its extensive ministry with singles. (Van Varner, "Singles in Our Society," *Guideposts* [November, 1975], pp. 16–18.) Though over 1500 are involved in this fellowship, a unique feature is small "Growth Groups" which last 16 weeks. In them singles "grapple with their own uniqueness, their relationships with other people, with God. They called the goal of those groups, 'Successful Singularity' " (p. 17).

7. Dietrich Bonhoeffer, *Life Together* (New York: Harper & Row, 1954 [originally published in Germany under the title of *Gemeinsames Leben*]), p. 110.

8. Recommended reading on building genuine relationships includes *No Longer Strangers* by Bruce Larson (Waco, Texas: Word Books, 1971), *Why Am I Afraid to Tell You Who I Am?* and *The Secret of Staying in Love* by John Powell (Niles, Illinois: Argus Communications, 1969, 1974), and *The Strong and the Weak* by Paul Tournier (Philadelphia: Westminster Press, 1963). Eph. 4:15–32 gives excellent guidelines for relationships with others, as does Phil. 2:1–7.

9. Virginia Mollenkott, "Jesus, Women and the Resurrection," *Eternity* (March 1975), p. 19.

10. Letha Scanzoni and Nancy Hardesty, *All We're Meant to Be* (Waco, Texas: Word Books, 1974). Excellent treatment on the single woman is given in chapter 12, "The Single Woman." Also recommended for a sensitive and probing treatment of the single life is Margaret Evening's *Who Walk Alone* (Downers Grove, Illinois: InterVarsity Press, 1974).

11. Francis Schaeffer, "No Little People, No Little Places," *No Little People* (Downers Grove, Illinois: InterVarsity Press, 1974), pp. 21–25.

12. Ryrie, *The Role of Women in the Church,* pp. 83–84, 142–43.

13. Richard J. Mouw, "Why Go to Church?" *The Reformed Journal* (March 1975), p. 24.

3.
The Church
and the Unmarried

Mark W. Lee

WHILE CONTROVERSY about traditional marriage has grown in intensity during recent years, little has been seriously written or said about the life of single adults. What has been popularly written and said must tend to embarrass serious single men and women—they may find themselves stigmatized by a stereotype which alleges that they are selfish, excessively affluent, sex-oriented, and irresponsible. Meaningful articles and books on the status of singles are beginning to appear but are not yet as definitive as writings on love and marriage. Many are the extensions of individual experiences, and some are defensive. The single adult is confronted with a nearly universal assumption—

MARK W. LEE is the president of Simpson College in San Francisco, a position he has held since 1970. Previously he taught speech and communication at Whitworth College, Spokane, and Northwestern College, Minneapolis. He is a graduate of Wheaton College (Ill.) and has a Ph.D. degree from the University of Washington. He is the author of *Our Children: Our Best Friends,* and his *Why Marriages Fail* is to be published soon. Dr. Lee is married and has four children and three grandchildren.

that marriage is to be preferred over single status. Even with
growing disillusionment about marriage, society has generally
held that normal adults were either married or wished to be.
Therefore, singleness is a temporary experience transitional to
marriage.

Marriage has grown in popularity if not in solidarity. Early
in the twentieth century 20 percent of Americans never married.[1] Currently, less than 10 percent will not marry. That
number represents a population equal to Canada's. With the
termination of the frontier dominated by single males and the
rise of world wars which made marriage attractive to men and
women, the percentage of singles declined. In war or with the
threat of war, a family man was less likely to be drafted, or if he
was drafted, his dependents received special benefits.

The trend may be turning again. Presently the number of
singles appears to be increasing in the population at the rate of
two million yearly. The increase is explained in part by
a general uncertainty about society, the extension of education
into the life span, disillusionment with marriage as it is commonly idealized, and a greater permissiveness in sexual activity,
making casual liaison a substitute for marriage. Many singles
report themselves to be unmarried but cohabiting as though
married. More persons have delayed or will skip marriage.
Some old impediments to marriage have grown larger. The
marriage gradient has become more complex in recent years,
that is, the tendency of men "to marry down" and women "to
marry up." [2] Women commonly enhance their own worth by
marrying men who are economically, socially and educationally
superior to themselves. Men see themselves as maintaining personal status in marrying women not as advanced as they are.
The differential should not be wide, they feel, but it is perceived.
As education and status of women improve, fewer women perceive men to be in advanced positions and fewer men perceive
women to be in lower.

While these changes were taking place, almost imperceptible shifts in population trends occurred. Many men remained in rural areas of the nation, particularly in the west. Single women moved in large numbers to population centers, especially to the megalopolitan areas. Men were not where the women could be found. And in upper age groups women outnumber men. Even if they wish to do so, some women can never marry. Men are too few, by several million, to go around.

One seldom-discussed reason for remaining single is that many persons choose not to marry. Remaining single is perceived by them to be a natural and fulfilling life style. One in three marriageable-age adults is single at any point in time. Many of these are divorced, widowed, or separated and will not be included in the purview of this chapter. The focus of this discussion is on the concerns of those adults who have not married, and may never do so.

Remaining single is as appropriate an option as being married. Because their status is appropriate, singles should be ministered to by the church in a manner as thorough and dignified as that which characterizes ministries to mother, father and dependent children.

Who Are the Unmarried?

When Jesus described the sanctity of marriage, his terms stimulated mild protest from his disciples (Matt. 19:3–12). They suggested that the high expectations of Jesus' idealism might cause persons to evade marriage. Jesus acknowledged that they were right and stated that acceptance of his view required maturity and insight. The privilege of remaining single was open to those who would choose it. And then he reviewed the reasons for remaining single:

For there are different reasons why men cannot marry: some because they were born that way; others because men made them that way; and others do not marry because of the Kingdom of heaven. Let him who can do it accept this teaching (Matt. 19:12, TEV).

Jesus suggested three basic reasons for remaining single: the circumstances (1) of birth, (2) of life, (3) of religious commitment. There is no compelling reason to believe that Jesus meant to be exhaustive with his list. However, if the references may be expanded somewhat from limited and common interpretations, all known reasons for remaining single are implicit in Jesus' words.

Persons May Have No Compulsive Need for Marriage

Jesus' reference to the circumstances of birth was acknowledgment that some persons are born physically incapable of sexual intercourse. Their sex organs will never become functional. As the congenitally blind person should not be mocked, neither should a person be treated insensitively who has been denied the function of sexual organs. Of course, other congenital problems not directly related to sex may prevent marriage.

There is no obvious reason why a man and a woman, both physically limited by birth, could not marry, unless frustration relative to physical intimacy would become excessively strong. If marriage is for companionship, for mutual growth, and for the larger purposes of sharing risks, the marriage might be well advised. So few persons are affected by congenital problems limiting marriage that the general population may not attach importance to the matter.

Jesus' reference to birth might be extended to physiological issues which the ancients would not know about. Differences in chemistry which affect the mental/emotional temperament of persons might cause intense interest in marriage with its relationships for some and little or no interest for others. Sexual drives for these latter are less demanding and readily manageable. This differential may account for the Pauline reference to a "gift," which will be discussed later.

The assumption on the part of active sex-oriented persons that all other men and women are compelled by the same drives is unproved. Society at large, however, presumes that sex drives are universal and the norm for human beings. If an individual seems to manage well without sex or marriage, that person is viewed with much skepticism. The general population finds it hard to believe that any significant segment will not seek sexual fulfillment. And the most satisfying fulfillment is affirmed to be in marriage.

Singles may become objects of prejudice because they are presumed to be out of norm, or if in norm they may appear as threats to the fidelity of marriages. A husband and wife may view each other as his and her property. The single, then, is a threat who may steal marital property. Enos Hawkinson has spoken to the problem:

> I have become convinced that our treatment of unmarried people is a symptom of our misunderstanding of Christian marriage. We do not, by marrying, become each other's property, complete with boundary surveys and signs reading, "No trespassing." That is indeed our practice, but it is not Christian; it is merely more of the acquisitive, possessive instinct so highly developed in our society.[3]

Any marriage counselor of experience has encountered women who were inordinately jealous of their husbands and suspicious of single women with whom their husbands held even the most casual conversation. Certainly husbands have taken offense at their wives for similar reasons. In the majority of all instances, possessiveness and concern about faithfulness were dominant. The fears were generally unfounded.

The difference between the status of marrieds and that of singles may be suggested by analogy. A chemical element has well-defined properties and is a basic substance—that is, it cannot be subdivided into simpler elements by chemical means. Elements combine to make compound substances to which new properties then pertain. The elements lose their independent identity in the compound. Hydrogen is a gas, as is also oxygen. Both are elements. Hydrogen is flammable, and oxygen aids burning. But chemically combined the two gases become a liquid—water—which inhibits burning.

In the same way, a single person functions as an element. He possesses his own special identity, his own properties. When two single people unite in marriage, a compound is formed— "the two have become one flesh." Each has given up elemental (single) life for compound (married) life. Each married person must surrender independent use of his/her elemental character, while the single person, as long as he/she chooses to remain single, may not presume to function in the compound relationship. No person, under God, may have it both ways. He or she is afforded options and should choose, but cannot morally and simultaneously engage the life of both forms.

Persons May Be Incapacitated for Marriage

Jesus' second reference in the Matthew text appears to refer to mutilation. Mutilation, more of men than women, was a common ancient practice which rendered slaves or servants incapable of marital intimacy. The assumption has generally been made that male eunuchs of ancient times were castrated. This protected the master's family or harem from sexual violation. Mutilation was also a form of punishment. And in our time, castration has been proposed as a means of social control. It has been tried on criminal or antisocial types who experience compulsive but objectionably sexual behavior.

Occasionally, accidents occur at birth. Because of accidents which have taken place during the process of circumcision, or other surgery, some male infants have been made impotent. In

several such instances sex changes have been surgically per-
formed.

But it seems to me this reference of Jesus may be extended to
the larger arena of human experience. There may be found
cultural and psychological influences which make marriage difficult for many men and women. Persons may become conditioned to resist or avoid relationships with the opposite sex
which could lead to marriage. Culture may have much to do
with either long delay or avoidance of marriage. The age at
which men marry in some societies, like that of Ireland, is later
than in America. The attitudes of the dominant church in
Ireland, economic conditions there, and paternal family style all
contribute to delayed marriage. In any developed society, economic depression tends to discourage early marriage.

Currently a new issue is being discussed. The emergence of
the women's liberation movement is alleged to have created
some fear or uncertainty about male-female relationships. Several counseling centers have encountered men who profess to
have no interest in sex in any mode of expression, and who
declare themselves to be without interest in women even apart
from sexual intimacy. This attitude may spring from other
causes than women's liberation. And some women have declared
themselves not only disinterested in sharing with men in marital
relationships, but also disinterested in men at all, and even in
rebellion against them. But what is unattractive to one segment
may be attractive to another. It should be acknowledged that
the new attitudes engendered by women's liberation are perceived to be preferable and stimulating to some men and
women.

Unhappy childhood homes, ill treatment of children by
family members or others, lack of education, influence of the
news media, and general societal changes—all these have conditioned many persons against the prospect of marriage. Counselors with extensive experience have encountered these persons

who are not likely to feel comfortable with the thought of marriage. Had the influences been moderated, they might have found marriage a fulfilling experience.

Persons may be influenced, after a period of successful marriage, by one or more negating factors. Those persons may find themselves unwilling or virtually incapable of continuing in the marriage relationship. They wish to be single and generally seek to have their marriages dissolved. This issue is commonly discussed among liberationists.

Persons May Be Spiritually Motivated to Refrain from Marriage

The choice to remain single is, for many, related to effective service for God. In the beginning Adam functioned singly, as the only one of his species. Femaleness was obvious in the animal world observed by that first man. The creation of Eve was subsequent to a period in which Adam thought about the world of his experience and worked in Eden's garden. He had the capacity to relate to God and find gratification there— as man is likely to do in eternity where they "neither marry, nor are given in marriage" (Luke 20:35, KJV).

The Scriptures portray an integrity of spiritual life in several persons who were single. Joseph in Potiphar's house maintained that integrity. John the Baptist, Mary and Martha with their brother Lazarus, all appear to have been single. Mary Magdalene and other women are not identified as belonging to families. Certainly Jesus was single. The Apostle Paul, whose early adult life continues as a matter of dispute relative to marital status, was unmarried during the period we know about him. His assertions about the matter imply that he remained unmarried for reasons which related to his spiritual commitment (1 Cor. 9:4–5).

All persons are single before marriage and will be separated or divorced or bereft unless their own death precedes. All persons live for a period of time as singles. Not all persons will be married, but all will live for a meaningful period as singles. This volume of experience implies the naturalness of the unmarried state. Certainly the Christian life and conduct which ought to characterize the believer is not qualitatively different for singles and marrieds. Only the marriage relationship is not part of the life of singles. For marrieds, the dual relationship provides a workshop for the practice of Christian virtues. Singles practice Christian virtues in other contexts.

The implication of Scripture is that when the choice of marital status is made there is also a gift which accompanies it so that each person is empowered to keep fidelity with his choice. Apparently the Apostle Paul, under the conviction that Jesus would soon redeem the physical world by his second coming, preferred celibacy for himself and others. He acknowledged that marriage is a normal estate and that, single or married, one required a gift, perhaps a natural endowment, for his choice (1 Cor. 7:7). Apparently one of the significant signs that one does not possess the gift to be single is the deep sense of sexual passion which might be interpreted as longing for a meaningful intimate relationship with a member of the opposite sex (1 Cor. 7:9). In any event, one's marital status should be determined by the exercise of the gift relative to it that one possesses.

The concept of the gift or natural endowment to be single has for centuries been used by the Catholic church in the selection of priests and nuns. Many applicants for the priesthood have been discouraged by their superiors from continuing on to their final vows because they lacked the endowment for celibacy. The break with celibacy by many Catholic clergy who leave the ministry to marry might well be matched by the number of Protestant ministers who leave pastorates because of their failing marriages.

Today, sociological research is widely controlled by those who are married and by scholars who confront an inordinate number of troubled singles. To judge unmarrieds on pathological cases is as objectionable as judging marriage on the record of separation and divorce. New studies with fresh approaches and larger samples may be needed to get at all the facts. Observation of Christian singles might provide a different profile than that which results from current materials. Christianity can fulfill human needs, regardless of marital status.

The gift discussed here may be self-control. Self-control requires one to be faithful to his choice of elemental (single) or compound (married) life.

It may be assumed that the gift for marriage status may be changed in a person. Counselors have worked with persons who have remained happily unmarried until the fourth or fifth decades of their lives. They may then marry and follow patterns of establishing family relationships. Many men and women, especially women, have lost their mates and lived the remainder of their lives fulfilled and alone. They practiced self-control in both situations. In Scripture, Anna is referred to as a woman who was married seven years and had been a widow for the rest of her eighty-four years. She devoted her time to spiritual exercises (Luke 2:36–37).

Ministry to the Unmarried

The church must minister to the needs of singles. In order to do so effectively, it must take the following seven actions:

1. *Recognize that single status is the appropriate available option to being married.* The Apostle Paul and other biblical writers did not visualize the church as a federation of families. Analysts might be hard pressed to prove that singles are more or less effective in Christian living than marrieds. Happy, mature Christian singles have accepted themselves, find meaningful relationships with their relatives or family substitutes, do not permit themselves to be separated from the mainstream of life activity, are unselfish, have more than average interest in culture and the arts, find meaningful fulfillment in their jobs, and

maintain appropriate social activity. They date, usually from a variety of persons to avoid any illusion or romantic commitment. They are humorous, interesting conversationalists, and are well aware of human drives. They are effective counselors and confront standard problems intelligently. During recent years a bachelor has been the most popular evangelical teacher on family life. And if Christian missions should be called upon to release single women missionaries serving around the world, the overseas enterprise of the church would become chaotic.

2. *Relate to the interests of singles.* Churches may be so tuned in to the interests of marrieds in family security and development, purchase of lands and houses, education and programs for youth, that little time or insight is left for singles. The interests of singles in personal development, culture and the arts, and the like, would, if given attention, improve the spiritual and intellectual life of the whole church. One is sometimes made aware that much of the banal culture in the church is pitched toward the tastes of children or youth. Parents accept the standard because they presume it holds their children in line until they grow up.

3. *Provide full opportunity for singles to act responsibly in the life of the church.* We let unmarried women become church secretaries or teachers of small children in Sunday school, and unmarried men become ushers. But why should they not become chairpersons of church boards, development officers, and the like? Singles may engage in Christian occupation and avocation without concern for the needs and comforts of mates. Unmarried Christian men and women appear to devote more time to their jobs and assignments than marrieds, are less concerned with financial rewards or recognition, and are more willing to do onerous chores. At the very least, singles should be identified equally with marrieds in the communion of the church. Single tend to perceive their status as a given, rather than as a matter of choice—they are single, have been single, and that is the way of it. If churches were to affirm their natural state life would be more gratifying.

4. Call upon all Christians to keep fidelity with biblical principles relative to personal conduct. Singles groups are sometimes criticized for shallowness or immorality revealed in pleasure-seeking, self-indulgence and, on occasion, illicit sex. Some of the sternest criticism has come from singles themselves. Church counselors have confronted allegations. Counselees often complain about the moral level of church singles subgroups they have encountered. For church-related singles organizations to succeed as Christian, limited taboos may be agreed upon and clear purposes adopted. Groups flounder when guidelines are not provided and taken seriously.

But the problems encountered among church marrieds may be just as open to censure. If one compares the problems of families encountered by counselors to those of singles, I doubt that one can make either set more reprehensible in one group. The church should speak to spiritual needs and values. The entire Christian population is the target. Minority groups within that population, when given equal treatment, may be expected to function at equal levels to their fellows.

5. Adjust the present focus of the church's ministry on the nuclear family. Most privileges in church and society appear to be provided for mothers, fathers, and dependent children. These occupy an inordinate quantity of the church's time, conversation and money. It is true that an exposition of Ephesians 5 affirms an analogy between Christ and the church, and the family. But this passage does not complete the story. The New Testament writers addressed their fellow Christians as *brother* and *sister*. The church is not a nuclear family, but a koinonia or community, a participation rather than an association.[4]

Certainly the nuclear family needs help. It seems to be disintegrating before our eyes. We are desperate for something to do. But my contention here is that singles may have been the objects of even greater neglect than the family. The church must focus on the whole task.

6. Activate programs which will meet the needs of singles.

The most common frustration for singles is loneliness.[5] Other complaints include omission of sex and parenthood, concealment of human emotions, and status.[6] A sentence or two on each of these needs will serve our purpose here.

Loneliness is not overcome until one shares with a "significant other" personal experiences and insights. Even so, loneliness is also a common complaint of married people. Sex drives become more intense in this age of conspicuous consumption. They may not have been as severe during the longer history of man. Also, the large amount of time and attention given to the subject of children both in conversation and in living may arouse a desire on the part of singles to have children of their own. Intense family orientation creates tension for nonfamily persons. Singles feel they must conceal sorrows, social interests and other personal matters. "Openness" is less open for singles. To express feelings is taken as evidence of unrequited desire. Marrieds are permitted a larger range of expression. A single person commonly confronts misunderstanding and prejudice which reduces social status. For example, unmarrieds, especially men, are paid less than marrieds. George F. Gilder stated that single men comprise 80 to 90 percent of most of the categories of social pathology.[7] The evidence of what is happening to singles at large in society is of concern here only insofar as the status of all singles is conditioned by the stereotype. The Christian single deserves equal privileges to those which differentiate a Christian family from one not Christian.

Singles do belong to their paternal families and generally try to meet their needs for giving and receiving love and approval by maintaining close ties with their families. Some seek family substitutes for these purposes and find them in the church. They should not withdraw from participation.

The church should offer classes, formal and informal, designed to serve the adult who is separated physically or psychologically from the nuclear family. Social programs and special projects should be provided, and the library ought to order books that will speak to their needs. Special counseling for problems of the unmarried ought to be offered, just as marriage and family counseling is offered. Leadership from singles ought to be cultivated. At present, married leaders often guide singles organizations. In addition, conferences for singles, participation in the affairs of the church, and recognition in publications might help to focus on the needs of unmarrieds from college age upward. Several nationally eminent churches, east and west, have introduced singles groups into their larger ministries. They have worked with limited literature to guide them. Each appears to have developed styles and characteristics original to itself.

In order to provide adequate ministries for singles, churches need to take into account where the singles are in their emotional life. Counselors describe four groupings of singles as they relate to marriage. Some singles wish to get married as a matter of preference. Most of these will. They proceed with their jobs, and involve themselves with society. They may dream, even fantasize about marriage, but they survive and refuse to lose the benefits of living because they are not married. They ultimately resolve the issue of their lives and are at peace. The church is greatly benefited by these people. Too little is known about happy singles.

Some singles will be married at any cost. They force themselves to accept mates significantly different in culture and conduct in order to be married. Perhaps they also sacrifice morals and integrity in order to ingratiate themselves and gain marriage. Unhappiness, disillusionment and failure commonly follow. And life may never get on track again. Many church young adults encounter such cross-cultural problems which ministers are called upon to help solve. This is a major issue.

Some singles are determined to remain single. For many their unmarried status is fulfilling and they are happy. They are able to disregard stereotypes which are sometimes used to characterize them, and are helpful and functioning members of society. Others, however, determine to remain single because of dislike or distrust of the opposite sex. Norman Bradburn, working with the National Opinion Research Center of the University of Chicago, found single men to be the unhappiest of all persons tested in the American society. He discovered that single women are more satisfied with their choice to remain unmarried. We do not know if some persons are unhappy because they are single or remain single because they are unhappy. We do know that many married persons are deeply unhappy, and that many singles are happy.

Some analysts claim that among singles there are many personality types which make difficult marriage partners. They wisely remain single. In his book, *Naked Nomads,*[8] George Gilder argues that "single males are losers." He describes the single state for males as almost wholly unsatisfactory. Much is written about the single male, and the critics presume that things would be better for him if he were married.

Most singles who become involved in social deviation are at ages which make them unsatisfactory as marriage risks. The problems presented by single males may be consequential to a mixture of youthful biological development and an environment which permits or encourages deviant behavior. The assumption that marriage corrects youthful male antisocial conduct or that the fault is related to single status are assumptions which require more competent analysis.

Some singles wish to remain single but maintain casual or periodic liaisons and share in both the elemental and compound experiences described earlier. This Playboy/Playgirl philosophy is not effectively defended in Christian circles, nor can it be. Nonetheless, the church is somewhat affected by that philosophy and should be prepared to assist persons who must confront the related issues of selfishness and irresponsibility.

7. *Build the church on Jesus Christ.* Many churches appear to be founded upon families. The ancient prejudices which denied rights to single men and women persist in church prac-

/

tice because the focus may be not on Christ but on the family unit, which seems more productive to the church in numbers, support and permanence. With all the importance of the family to church and society, to concentrate virtually all the church's resources to that ministry does not achieve God's purpose.

Biblical truth ought to be applied to individual needs rather than to the family when the individual application is the most appropriate. And, in Christian humility, marrieds may need to ask forgiveness for their failure to be sensitive and to empathize with singles who, under God, become what they were meant to become.

Singles will need some activism. In a spirit of forbearance they need to apply appropriate pressure on the church and its ministers. They will succeed as they match their activism with creative and Christlike lives.

At this juncture in history much more is known about marriage and the family than the unmarried and the church. If the differential is to be reduced, it will be done in part by responsible persons who are married and have broken down barriers to understanding. The additional part must be assumed by singles who will prevail as exemplary Christian men and women.

Notes

1. George R. Bach and Peter Wyden, *The Intimate Enemy* (New York: Avon, 1975), p. 35.

2. Alfred J. Prince, "Why Some Never Marry," *Spokesman-Review Sunday Magazine* (November 9, 1969), p. 7.

3. Enos Hawkinson, "Remember the Singles," *The Covenant Companion* (October 1, 1972), p. 7.

4. Ralph P. Martin, "Church," in *Baker's Dictionary of Christian Ethics,* Carl F. H. Henry, ed. (Grand Rapids, Michigan: Baker Book House, 1973), p. 373.

5. Joyce Brothers, "Coping with Loneliness, Drugs, Alcohol, Anxiety," *Harper's Bazaar,* March 1975.

6. Paul Tournier, *The Adventure of Living* (New York: Harper & Row, 1965), pp. 131 ff.

7. George F. Gilder, *Sexual Suicide* (New York: Bantam Books, 1974), pp. 5–6.

8. George F. Gilder, *Naked Nomads: Unmarried Men in America* (New York: Quadrangle Books, 1974).

4.
Learning to Live Alone:
The Divorced Person
and the Church

Virginia McIver

WHAT DOES IT MEAN when divorce happens to you? How do
you feel? What are your needs? Who do you turn to for help? I
used to think divorce only happened to someone else, to the
worldly, not to a Christian. But it did happen to me! I can only
speak out of my own experience, so mine is a story of how I
felt, what I needed, how these needs were met, and how the
church can help others who are divorced.

My Personal Experience

I grew up in a Christian home and accepted Christ as my
Savior when very young. When college time came, I chose a
Christian college and there fell in love with a young man who
said he was a Christian. We married, went to graduate school

VIRGINIA McIVER is a graduate of John Brown University, Siloam
Spring, Arkansas, with a degree in sacred music. She and her three
children live in Houston, Texas, where she works for the Baptist Book
Store and teaches piano students.

and the army, and then we settled down to work with an oil company and raise our family.

Our family was active in our church. In fact we were there every time the doors were open. We sang in the choir, taught in Sunday school, sponsored youth groups, worked with children's choirs, and did whatever there was to do. Dick served as a deacon and finally was elected chairman.

Then one day my world fell apart. My husband told me he did not love me and had not for years. He also confessed that he had never believed in a personal God, and that his prayers, testimonies, etc., were a part of the game he was playing. He could play it no longer, so after almost twenty-two years of marriage it was all over.

What do you feel when you find yourself alone for the first time in years, when the responsibility of a home and children is suddenly yours alone? I was afraid—afraid I could not find a job, afraid I could not handle two teenage boys, afraid the children would not be happy in a home with just a mother.

For a time life hardly seemed worth living. The children needed me and needed to be cared for, but as much as I loved them there were times when I wished I could die and not have to face the future.

Loneliness closed in. There was no man coming home at five o'clock to fix supper for. There was no adult companionship, no one to help decide whether a child was sick enough to call a doctor. I missed having someone with whom to share my children's heartaches and joys, someone to fix their broken toys.

I think the hardest feelings to handle were those of anger, bitterness, jealousy, vindictiveness. I wondered why this had happened and could not understand why he had not expressed some of his feelings earlier so we could have sought professional help. It was hard after so many years of knowing his daily activities not to know what he was doing, how he was, and if he was seeing another woman. At times there was a feeling of needing to hurt him, to get even in some way for the hurt he had caused me.

I went through a period of time when I too wondered if there really was a God. If I could believe what the Bible said, then I knew I could depend on him, and that the kids and I would be all right. The thought of the possibility of facing the future without God was terrifying.

I had always had a great deal of respect for my ex-husband's opinions. Now he was telling me there was no God who cared about me. But as I saw God work in our lives, as needs were met and jobs found, and as I began to see a little of the pattern God was weaving, I knew from experience that the promises he made were true, and that I could depend on him.

My present relationship with Dick is a good one. We can talk about most anything and feel comfortable doing so. We work together for the benefit of the children. I no longer feel bitterness or anger. There will always be regrets and memories that hurt a little; on special days there will probably be a few tears, but the hurt is now minimal.

I am very human and I had all the typical reactions. Why have I been able to come through this experience with a feeling of contentment, of joy, of freedom and excitement for living? Of course time does help heal, but the complete wholeness I feel has to be the work of the Holy Spirit in my life. I began to realize that there is nothing haphazard about God's plan for us. When we come to the point where we let God have control of our lives, then he can use the circumstances of life for his purpose—to make us more like him.

As I learned to view each event from this perspective, the healing process began. I also discovered a desire to show that being a Christian does make a difference in how you live, even in the most difficult of circumstances.

My needs were met, not by "the church," but by people in the church. A few friends from "before" called. Others wrote notes or called expressing their love and support. But the Lord sent four special people who, each in her own way, contributed to my recovery. I also had a very wonderful family who, even though at a great distance, came, called, wrote, and most important, prayed. And through it all I felt the support and love of my children.

What did these friends do? They called, they came to visit, they took me to lunch, and I was included in some of their social activities. They cared about me, they loved me, they listened when I needed to talk. But most important, they showed me the necessity of a strong faith in God and helped me realize that God is concerned with and wants to be a part of every event in my life, even those unrepaired toys and chairs.

Something else that was a great deal of help to me was a share group and a Bible study. These were not organized by the church, rather by these friends who felt the groups would meet a need in their lives. They not only provided fellowship with other adults but also helped me learn to express some of my feelings and needs. I felt accepted and loved and strengthened through this sharing of joys and problems and praying together about them.

They suggested books for me to read, and this widened my horizons. In the Bible and books I found comfort and strength from fellow strugglers as they related their faith walk, though their situations were most often different from mine.

My children's needs were met by the church. They continued in Sunday school and all other church activities. Though few approached them with offers of help or questions concerning their well-being, they felt no change in the attitudes of friends or teachers and felt accepted and as much a part of the church as always.

The Church and the Divorced Person

Let us turn now to some positive thoughts on how the church can meet the needs of the divorced. First there needs to be a change in the attitudes of the staff and church members toward persons who are involved in divorce. Why is it that when there is a death, people rush right in with visits, food, and offers of help? Yet, when a person is facing divorce—the death of a marriage—many people stay away. They don't know what to say, or are afraid of intruding. Yet this is a time when people are desperately needed. The reassurance that you are still acceptable, not someone undesirable, and that you are worthy of friendship, helps to restore a feeling of self-worth.

The absence of needed support leads one to feel condemned by those in the church, whether this is actually their attitude or not. Jesus never condemned those in difficulty; one prime example was his reply to the adulteress (John 8:11). Often when I think of the demands made on the time and energies of the clergy, I am reminded that Jesus said, "They that are whole have no need of a physician, but they that are sick" (Matt. 9:10, ASV).

In Galatians 6:1–2 we read, "Brethren, even if a man be overtaken in any trespass, ye who are spiritual, restore such a one in a spirit of gentleness; looking to thyself, lest thou also be tempted. Bear ye one another's burdens, and so fulfil the law of Christ" (ASV). The picture of the church painted in Ephesians does not show a single one of God's children as being neglected, ignored or looked down upon when they are in despair. Paul states in the fourth chapter that God gave different abilities to those in the church for the purpose of ministering "unto the building up of the body of Christ; till we all attain unto the unity [maturity] of the faith" (Eph. 4:12–13, ASV).

In recent years there have been some strides made in the church's ministry to single adults. Many churches have classes for them and some even have a staff member whose ministry is only to single adults. All of this is important. But perhaps the greatest need and the one most neglected in the church is a ministry to couples when they are separated, facing divorce, and making adjustments during the time immediately after a divorce —a period of intense trauma and emotional upheaval.

At such times a visit from the pastor or a staff member is a must to determine what is needed and to let the person know that the church is concerned and wants to help. It is not wise to wait for a call from the person facing divorce; the pastor should go as soon as the situation is known. Perhaps some counseling is needed or a referral to a professional counselor.

People are often hesitant about letting it be known that they have marital problems. But with their approval the pastor can share the information with a Sunday school superintendent or a teacher so these can phone, can offer help and pray.

Some go through a divorce with no one to help them, to listen to them, to be a friend to them. I'd like to suggest a group of people, listeners, whom the Lord has called to minister in this way. The pastor, knowing the situation, could choose one, who would not only be a friend and listener, but would be able to give spiritual guidance as well.

Ideally perhaps, these people would be other single adults who, having gone through a similar experience, could more easily understand the problems. However, I feel the only real qualification need be someone called by the Lord who knows how to love.

After helping a divorced person through these critical first days, the church should be prepared to suggest some additional helps. This could be in the form of small groups or seminars which would meet *practical, emotional,* and *spiritual* needs. Small groups lend themselves to building long-term relationships. Here the divorced person would get to know other people, feel accepted by them, and in this atmosphere be able to regain or develop the self-confidence needed to adjust to a new role and make a new life for self and for children.

Some people seem to feel that being a Christian means little more than being saved from hell. When I found myself alone with no man to depend on, it was a frightening experience. I needed to be involved in serious Bible study to be reminded that God loved me as I was and was concerned about me in the day-to-day problems I faced; that he had a plan for my life and wanted to be involved in all aspects of it, and that I could depend on him for help. And through the Scriptures I needed to be reminded that there could be no room in my life for hatred, unmercifulness, or grudges (Matt. 5:43–46; Luke 6:36; Eph. 5:31).

A real need for many divorcées is to find their identity. Many women have been content to be wife and mother, and have no other identity. After a divorce, such a woman must find out exactly who she is by finding out and proving what she can do. This often requires entering the labor market for the first time or reentering after many years out of the business world. Many who marry right out of college have never developed a skill to earn a living and must start at this late time in life to do so. This is very frustrating and one needs constant support and reassurance from those who love her that she can make it. A large part of this could and should come from her Christian acquaintances.

It is also important to verbalize the emotions and hostilities one feels at this time. Often it takes a lot of "talking through" before one can really get to the root of the problem and understand something about oneself and the facts that led to the divorce.

In sharing experiences it helps to find that you are not the only one who faced a particular problem. And in talking about problems you learn how others have dealt with them. There is no one better qualified, nor should there be one more ready to lend a listening ear and loving heart than the people of God.

Since most women usually depend on their husbands to take care of such things as the car, repair jobs around the house, etc., there are many practical needs in the life of the divorcée that the church can minister to. Seminars or even one-to-one counseling to discuss the following subjects could help meet many of these needs.

1. Purchase and care of a car
2. Insurance
3. Income tax
4. Various aspects of home maintenance
5. Several psychological aspects such as
   a. Relationship with ex-husband
   b. Problems of children in divorce
   c. Guilt feelings

In years past it was normal and rather expected that when one had the misfortune of being divorced, he or she would disappear from all the old familiar circles—including church. This is no longer expected, but is perhaps still the most natural reaction. Those who are just divorced do not seem to fit anywhere. If they have been a part of a Sunday school class, they may feel comfortable there for a while. But they soon realize that their needs and problems are no longer the same, and since social activities are planned around couples, they just don't go. The logical move is to go to a single adult class if the church has one, or to drop out of Sunday school if it does not.

But it is not as easy as it sounds to make the change. I felt comfortable being a single in the married world. Having been a part of that world for so long I found it most difficult making the change to the single adult class, but I knew it had to be made. It was only because of a lot of encouragement on the part of a few singles that I finally made the change. And it was much later before I felt a part of the class.

It is often thought that a person goes to a single adult class to find a mate, and this may be true. But more important is the need to be with people who have been through a similar experience, and who accept divorcées without looking down on them. The need for a social life is important and necessary and should be a part of the class. It needs to be co-ed so people can again learn to build casual relationships with the opposite sex.

Perhaps a church feels it does not have enough singles to start a class. But once a class is going, and if it has something to offer, it will draw other singles. I'd like to suggest this as an opportunity for outreach, as some non-Christians will be attracted to the church because of the class. There can be a problem of too wide an age span, and ideally the class should be structured so each person finds himself with people of similar age and experience. This will greatly enhance the ministry of the members to one another.

Singles need to be more involved in the total life of the church. Just because you are divorced does not mean you no longer are qualified to serve. The same talents and qualities of leadership are still there and need to be utilized. If there is an unaccepting attitude and lack of understanding, if people—particularly the church staff—fail to reach out to the divorced person, chances are the divorced person will never become greatly involved in the total church program. Many remain on the fringes and volumes of time and talents are lost from his kingdom's work.

Most of what I have said has been directed toward meeting the needs of the woman who remains in her church after divorce. Of course, the divorced man would have some of the same needs plus others, such as adjusting to living alone, the responsibility of an apartment, building a relationship with his children while seeing them infrequently, perhaps leaving "their" church to make a place for himself in a new church with new people. And more and more these days, fathers are being given custody of the children, so that they are experiencing the problems of being both father and mother.

I feel that most churches fail in ministering to the one who stays, but more dramatically they fail the partner who drops out of sight after the divorce. Often such a person is ostracized, or at best ignored, like a common criminal. How we regard this one's relationship to Christ is immaterial. The divorced mate is facing perhaps the greatest need of his or her whole life and we have a unique opportunity to be a minister of God's love and acceptance.

Can you imagine this person's disillusionment (that may turn into bitterness) toward the church and Christians? It should not come as a surprise if they completely turn their back on God. Then someone will have the tedious task of loving them back some day.

The divorced person is needed and can have a marvelous ministry in the church. Furthermore, the Christian who is divorced has every right to expect the church to make an effort to meet his or her needs, rather than ignoring them.

To summarize, the divorced person needs spiritual guidance, love, and acceptance. By providing Bible study, counseling and fellowship the church can, as it must, effectively minister to divorced persons and their families.

For Further Reading

Carothers, Merlin. *Power in Praise*. Plainfield, N.J.: Logos International, 1971.

Russell, A. J., ed. *God Calling*. Old Tappan, N.J.: Fleming H. Revell, 1972.

Schaeffer, Edith. *L'Abri*. Wheaton, Ill.: Tyndale, 1969.

Stewart, Suzanne. *Divorced! I Wouldn't Have Given a Nickel for Your Chances*. Grand Rapids, Mich.: Zondervan, 1974.

Taylor, Jack. *The Key to Triumphant Living*. Nashville: Broadman Press, 1971.

5.
The Formerly Married: The Church's New Frontier

Britton Wood

THE PEOPLE OF God are on the edge of one of the greatest adventures the church has ever known. We are beginning to take seriously all persons—particularly the divorced, widowed, and separated adults—in our midst. Ministry with and to these formerly married persons is the church's new frontier.

These formerly married persons represent a segment of adult society that has, up to now, been virtually ignored by churches. We have entered into a new era with the widowed and the divorced, when remaining single is a viable life style option. It's O.K. to be a single adult today.

The church has in the main been composed of married adults since the first century. Not until the 1960s have we been forced

BRITTON WOOD is the minister to college students and single adults at Park Cities Baptist Church in Dallas, Texas. Previously he was Baptist Student Union director at North Texas State, and director of religious activities at U. of Corpus Christi. He is a graduate of Hardin-Simmons University and has the B.D. and M.R.E. degrees from Southwestern Baptist Theological Seminary. He is married and the father of three girls.

to accept the reality of an increasing number of single persons—especially those who were formerly married.

Today the vision of the church needs to be enlarged to include the single adult as the church's new frontier. We need to see the church as two-thirds two-adult family units (married adults) and one-third one-adult family units (single adults), because one out of three adults in our society is single.

Other than single persons who have never married because of choice or lack of choice, persons are single due to death of spouse (widowhood), death of a marriage relationship (divorce), or a dying marriage (separation).

Difficulties in Ministering to the Formerly Married

The local congregation of believers often finds it difficult to minister to formerly married adults for several reasons.

The formerly married tend to blame God for their present marital status. This feeling of "God doing me in" comes from an inaccurate understanding of prayer, of God's will, and a lack of willingness to accept responsibility for all that occurs in one's life. Many persons plant seeds of personal destruction in a marriage relationship and are surprised when the seeds bear fruit. It is not uncommon for most persons to want to blame someone else for the things that are not working right in their lives.

The divorced adult feels guilty because the official word from the church regarding divorce is "thou shalt not." If divorced persons feel this guilt much at all, a sense of alienation and utter failure in relation to the church permeates their lives. Frequently I have talked with divorced persons about becoming involved or visiting the single adult groups of my church, and they have been hesitant to come until I say that we do not hang signs on them in large letters that say "Divorced," nor do we ask them for their "reason for being single." Our concern is that the divorced person, or any single for that matter, be accepted as he or she comes. We want broken lives to be healed and to become more fully the lives God through Christ wants them to become. We must practice "forgiving one another, as God in Christ forgave" us (Eph. 4:32, RSV). The issue is not whether persons should or should not divorce. God's intention in marriage is consistent, and the church should continually uphold the ideal of one man and one woman as long as both persons live. The fact is however that people are divorced and will continue to divorce. The church must be concerned about what we do to minister to these broken lives.

The formerly married usually feel out of place in most churches because adequate programing has not developed to meet their needs. Although changes are occurring rapidly, many churches are programed to meet the needs of the two-adult family units (married adults). Many married persons lack the sensitivity or the awareness to understand that ministry which is healthy for married persons may not be equally healthy for single adults. For instance, if a married ladies class is going to have a class social, the usual announcement emphasizes that each member is to "be sure and bring your husband." The mind-set of the church generally does not consider the formerly married person's situation or feelings. Single adults and married adults have some similar needs but they also have needs that are unique and must be cared for in different ways.

The formerly married resent the attitude of many married adults that reflects a superior-inferior kind of relating. Many persons who are married feel that the most important way to help the single person is to find them a suitable marital partner, and they find it inconceivable that some single adults choose to be single. Persons in the two-adult family units often feel that the single adult has not "arrived" until he is married or, to put it another way, has become "exactly like us married folk." Some married adults find the single adult life style threatening to the married adult life style because of the "everyone should want to get married" attitude held by many married adults. Another reason why the single adult life style can be threatening to a married couple is that the husband may fear his wife will want more freedom than she has in their marriage, or vice versa. It is also possible that a competitiveness with a single adult friend can occur for the mate of the married partner.

Church leadership is often uncomfortable with the responsibility of styling a program that meets the needs of single adults. Most churches are inadequately staffed even to meet the needs of two-adult families. It is not surprising that they are reluctant to jump into a whole new arena of ministry. But I am happy to observe a growing awareness and willingness on the part of many pastors and religious educators to expand the ministry of the local congregation to include the single adults. .

Concerns of the Formerly Married

The concerns of the formerly married are varied and vast. They cannot all be adequately developed at this point, but calling attention to some of them will challenge many in church leadership to explore more fully these concerns with their local communities of believers.

The concerns of the widowed adult are somewhat different from those of the divorced adult. For both the divorced and the widowed the death of the relationship is accompanied by the process of coping and understanding. Both need time to adjust to this death, but the widowed have more help from society and do not have to cope with the presence of the ex-spouse.

The process of divorce begins in a marriage when there is no longer trust, and when a growing isolation or lack of sharing is allowed to grow into resentment and hate. It continues with a growing separateness which may or may not include physical separation. At this point the erosion of the marriage begins to show itself to friends and family members. Divorce becomes a final reality through the legal process, but this may occur long before it is emotionally accepted as reality by the divorced individual.

The death of a spouse can come abruptly with no warning at all and leave the widowed in a state of shock. The coping process for the widowed is generally slow and takes place after the death of the spouse. If the death process is not immediate, the widowed person has time to lower the guilt level by expressing love and care during the dying process.

The concerns of the widowed and the divorced adult are similar in several ways.

Coping with being alone. Family oriented society has provided little help for the single adult. In many cases we have added dimensions of isolation from the two-adult family units by having apartments for singles only, singles bars, singles clubs and very few organizations which bring single and married adults together in our social milieu. Aloneness is unique to single adults whereas loneliness is not. Another way of stating "single adults" could be "alone adults." It is often difficult to cope with being alone as a single because of the pressure to marry as life's only fulfillment option. Creative efforts need to be made for the single adult to live alone well. The continuing education programs in today's universities offer many exciting and creative studies that single adults find challenging and fascinating.

Caring for self. When one's marital status is changed from married to widowed or divorced, a great loss of identity often follows. The self-confidence of the formerly married is often very low due to failure in marriage or rejection in death. Many times single adults attempt to overcome low self-esteem with excessive activity or by becoming selfish and intolerant of persons and situations which do not please them, or withdrawing from other persons by staying at home. When a person does not like or accept himself or herself, it is seldom possible to relate well to others. Unfortunately, the single person who does not like himself tends to try various solutions which are unhealthy, such as liquor, drugs, or perhaps even suicide. If God through Christ can express his acceptance of us "in that while we were yet sinners Christ died for us" (Rom. 5:8, KJV), could we not at least begin to accept who we are, too?

Choosing a direction in life. Although the choices in life have already been formed to some degree by the time a person is adult, the "suddenly" single person has to begin a new direction as to life style, vocation, or meaning in life. Women who were married and not working outside the home must begin to function adequately in a vocation. Often the formerly married woman is not equipped professionally because of lack of interest, children, or putting her husband through school. One difficult aspect of choosing a direction in life is that many formerly married persons thought they had already made that choice. Now that they are single again they dislike having to start all over.

Companionship with other single adults. Our society has up to this point provided very few outlets for single adult peer group friendships that are healthy. As a result, many men and women become so desperate for companionship that they will pay $250 to $500 to join a singles club and be "included" in some social events. Bar-hopping becomes a method for meeting potential companions. At times, panic overrides Christian teachings, producing the feeling that one *must* meet someone whatever the consequences are. The church can provide one of the few opportunities for single adults to meet in a nonthreatening environment. In a nonthreatening situation any single person can visit with or initiate conversations with another single adult without having to feel like the initiator is flirting or wants a date with that particular individual.

To encourage this kind of environment, single adults generally limit dating to nonchurch activities. It becomes easier to develop friendships with all persons present rather than limiting them solely to those who seem interesting enough to date. One result of this approach is the great sense of family and caring for and about one another. Some very deep friendships are forming among the single adults in the church where I am single adult minister to the level of sharing joys and sorrows because they know their friends care what happens in each life. Good marriages do emerge from good friendships. In one single adult department alone, twenty-five persons married within a six-week period, twenty-two of whom met in the department.

When single adults have opportunity to be friends, they are free to be themselves. When they are free to be themselves, their true attractiveness and uniqueness comes out. A friend of mine has said that we need to become aware of who we are, and when we let people know us that way, then they can forgive us for what we are not.

Concern for the children. Many formerly married persons are parents. The one-parent family has many adjustments to make and many pressures from the two-parent families as to the care of their children. At times these children tend to be excused when there is a discipline problem. "What can you expect?" society says; "her parents are divorced." Unfortunately, we put undue pressure on one-parent families and far too little on two-parent families. Single parents often become tired of parenting. They are exhausted from the twenty-four-hour-a-day parent pressure with no help from the ex-spouse. My contention is that if the church can help the parent care for his/her own personhood, encourage him/her to be involved in the single adult ministry where understanding friends are, and give God a chance to work in his/her life, then parenting can become bearable and begin to be fun. The church can assist greatly by having two-parent families available on various occasions for babysitting purposes so the single parent can go on a retreat or a singles conference. This kind of caring contribution helps the single adults to know that the whole church cares and chooses to be a part of this new frontier.

The religious education program of the church needs to educate all workers to be sensitive to the needs of children of single parents and yet not treat the children differently from the children of two-adult family units. Special seminars or share groups for single parents can be most helpful in the cope-ability of parents.

Commitment to Christ. Many problems occur in all lives if commitment to God in Christ is omitted. Being a formerly married person receiving too much advice at times and not enough at other times can blur the issues quite thoroughly. A consistent prayer life that seeks God's guidance is difficult even for two-adult families where each partner can encourage the other, but when one is alone the difficulty is greater. The absence of a caring person to encourage formerly marrieds underscores the importance of the Christian community of single adults. Much encouragement for personal Christian living can take place in a single adult group. One of the reasons single men are more frequently found in bars rather than churches is that they have not been confronted with the manliness of their commitment to Christ. Men have difficulty seeing the Christian faith in the midst of the distorted models of Christianity generally available to them.

One's commitment to Christ can make the difference for single adults as they attempt to face realistically all areas of their lives.

The Challenge of the New Frontier

The formerly married are definitely the challenge of the new frontier for the church today. It is imperative that church leadership consider wisely the approaches of ministry to single persons. Single adults will help the church become more dynamic than it has been in the past because of a new awareness of persons, a new willingness to be honest in interpersonal relationships, and a forgiving spirit among believers who are becoming more vulnerable in their relationships.

Some of the challenges for the church to consider in response to the formerly married are highly significant.

1. The church must provide channels of healthy relationships for younger single persons (ages eighteen to twenty-five). Young adults need encouragement to become productive persons who know who they are, and to postpone marriage until they have been on their own for a few years. The opportunities for short-term (two years or less) Christian service, the freedom to travel for both men and women, and the growing acceptance for young women to develop their own professional expertise will continue to enlarge the "postpone marriage" crowd among young adults. Recent research indicates that the best time to marry is age twenty-seven to thirty-one for men and age twenty-five for women.[1] The highest divorce rate comes from teenage marriages (one-half end in divorce) and the lowest divorce rate is in marriages that begin after age twenty-five.

Many churches provide activities and leadership for high school and college-aged youth, but few care for the single person after college days. It is generally assumed that by age twenty-two or so, most single adults will marry. In our church we have approximately four hundred fifty single adults between the ages of twenty-one and thirty, many of whom are not yet ready to get married (although attitudes shift somewhat among the three hundred fifty single adults in the thirty-one to sixty age group). These persons are not in a limbo period of their lives. They need opportunities to be the church now and to have valid ministries that form an accepting community for singles. Celibacy needs to be emphasized once again as a valid life style option for the formerly married as well as the never married single person. The person who is newly single due to death or divorce and the new single in town need a community of singles with whom to relate.

The church has worked diligently to care for married adults. Let us care equally for our single adults. Single adults want to be the church and want to take that responsibility seriously.

They have the ability and interest to take charge of their peer group activities, curriculum planning, church committees, personal witnessing with other singles, work or mission projects, planning for retreats, singles conferences, Bible study groups, mission organization leadership, church school Bible teachers, leaders of choral groups in the church, technical assistance with audio-visual aids, television, and recording equipment, and many other areas of need in the institutional church. The redeeming power of the Holy Spirit continues to channel capable single adults into the ministry of the church.

2. The church must reconsider its attitude to divorced persons. We need healthier ways to care for persons going through divorce. I find I can no longer be silent when I learn that a friend is having marital problems or is in the process of divorce. I am not so much interested in the details of the divorce as I am interested in the person in the divorce. I can't change anything that has happened, but I can care and be a friend in the midst of the changes that are occurring. As one divorced friend said, "What really matters is what *happens* to what happens to me."

How can we as the church assist divorced persons to have a healthier transition from married to single life with less trauma and loss of identity? The church can respond well to the widowed adult at the time of death of spouse, but says or does little to and for the divorced person. Unfortunately, the church is not generally aware of marital problems in a particular marriage until it is past the point of no return. One married man in a church in another city shared with me regarding his own marital problems that he could not share any of these concerns with his Sunday school class members, but he could share with some of his friends (indicating persons outside the church family).

A support group in the church for caring, listening and sharing of insights regarding divorce can be most helpful. Such a group can take different forms. It may consist of three to eight formerly married persons who are brought together by the minister or single adult leader. The purpose of the group is to share common feelings of hurt, to discuss and pray about steps to be taken from this point on, and to continue to meet on a week-to-week basis until this kind of support is no longer needed. A support group may last four to six weeks only. It may meet at night or during the noon hour or another convenient time. It can also be composed of married couples who have worked through their own problems.

3. The church must assist all formerly married persons with friendships which can give insight regarding finances, all kinds of decision making, vocational guidance, the process of grief, and spiritual nurturing in the midst of suffering. The church can have an employment information service for the single adults who are in between jobs, which will also provide counsel for those who feel they need to change professions. Many times getting the "right" vocational position frees one to relate to God better. This area of need is an excellent way to involve persons in the two-adult families with the concerns of the one-adult families.

4. The church must recognize that the presently married can learn much from the formerly married that will enrich their marriages. Every marriage relationship is vulnerable and can potentially end in divorce. With divorce as the one alternative least preferred for any marriage, the presently married should renew and update their marriage covenants. Church life must include some marital growth groups and other preventive maintenance for presently married adults. Small marital growth groups (four to eight couples) have met with a minister or a Christian psychologist for eight weeks discussing books like *The Intimate Marriage* or *The Miracle of Dialogue*.[2] Let the presently married become more honest about life as married adults so the nonmarried can become aware that conflicts exist in marriage and these conflicts can be worked through. Christian married persons who have tensions in their marriages but do not acknowledge them in valid situations limit their credi-

bility with the single adults who can see the flaws because they
have become aware of similar flaws in their former situation.

Married adults need some general advice as to what to do
when a friend is having marital problems. Also they need some
specific advice as to steps to take, books to read, or suggestions
for marriage counselors. A dialogue with the formerly married
persons on the subject "What I wish someone would have told
me before I married (assuming I would have listened)" could
be most educational and practical.

5. The church must encourage presently married persons to
accept the responsibility for being the unique couple they are,
with all their good points and imperfections. This will release
them from having to be an example couple for all to follow. We
need many models of couples in marriage rather than some un-
real examples which are not authentic because the people are
not free to be themselves. A good example of what I mean is
the response I received from a couple whom I asked to teach in
one of the single adult departments. Both husband and wife
felt they were still working on their relationship with each
other and with God. I told them that I preferred persons who
were still concerned about relationships and who didn't have
everything worked out already. Those who have it all worked
out are not learners. This is not to imply that some persons who
are "putting it all together" are not helpful or do not continue
to be learners. Single adults need learners or disciples to lead
them.

6. The church must recognize that all single adults are not
the same or at the same level of personal and spiritual development. It is impossible to minister to single adults adequately
with only one approach. I find that single adults tend to be in
one of three developmental stages: (1) Low self-esteem, or an
unhealthy concern for self. This level requires biblical insights
built on God's love, acceptance, forgiveness and reconciliation.
(2) Healthy self-esteem which includes the concerns of develop-

ing an identity and understanding one's unique gifts, and internalizing biblical teachings such as in the Sermon on the Mount and Paul's teachings regarding the fruit of the Spirit. (3) A healthy concern for others, which includes an understanding of the mission of the church, witnessing training, community mission projects and studying biblical suggestions regarding one's attitude in giving, sharing, and self-denial. We try to be sensitive in curriculum planning to include all three stages so as to meet the needs of all our single adults.

We need to allow for the fact that some single adults participate in single adult programs for reasons other than spiritual development. Some of our single adults have been part of our single adult game night crowd for a long time and eventually attend Sunday school or a retreat. In time, some of these persons have professed Christ and become active participants in our church. Single adults need to have the freedom to be involved in the church on their own commitment level. Some single adults remain on the attender only level, others become members of the Sunday school, and a good number choose to identify more completely through church membership.

7. The church must recognize that single adults who do participate in the life of the church are to be commended for their efforts. Unlike married adults, who have someone to encourage their participation and to attend church with and who also find a climate of acceptance in the married adult Sunday school, single adults need quite a lot of determination and discipline to be involved in the church. They are moving against the trend being set by other single adults, and in many churches they do not have an accepting group to welcome them.

Perhaps they can be encouraged by giving them more opportunities of responsibility in the life of the church. Single adults are actively involved in all aspects of church leadership and church committees at our church. They are very responsible and provide healthy ideas for our church as a whole to consider. Some have responded to God's call to vocational Christian service. Many have become active sharers of the Good News of Christ where they work, live, and in the social areas of their lives.

8. The church must recognize the importance of family in the lives of single adults. Many formerly married persons have become severed from family relationships and need a warm, accepting, caring family of single adults who understand what they have been through. The acceptance of single adults from the two-adult family units can assist in the healing process. It is important to note that single adults, whether formerly married or not, begin to relate to the whole family of God more readily if there is a small group of Christian brothers and sisters who help them feel accepted. It is generally easier for the formerly married to have a base group from which to relate to the whole.

Help on the Frontier

Much more could be said about the formerly married being the church's new frontier. Let us begin to express the belief that the church is the best avenue of help and health for the single person, especially the formerly married.

The church is the only institution that is styled to care for and welcome all persons regardless of where they are at any point in their lives. It is the character of the church to be forgiving and to be personal. The nature of the church is to provide spiritual growth for persons of all ages—and persons of all ages are part of the church. Most available group situations are peer-group oriented. The church provides peer group activities but it is also cross-peer-group oriented. Recently a cross-peer group of believers from the church where I serve went on a week-long mission project to Juarez, Mexico, to help build a mission and lead in Bible schools. The group was composed of junior high, high school, college, single and married persons. The warmth of the Spirit of God permeated the group and there were no discipline problems. Each age group either looked up to someone else or felt that they were being looked to as more mature, and God blessed the witness of this group. Each person paid his own way in this great experience.

The formerly married are fighting for their lives to be healthy and growing persons. They will, with or without the help of the church, attempt to have their needs filled. The people of God must not let this challenge be assumed by lesser lights in our world.

One of our single adults, Misty Stewart, expresses very well the feeling many formerly married persons have when they begin to consider the Christian alternative for their lives.

It Starts with a Breeze

I'm on the way to an
  Experience

I'm afraid
  I'm worried
    I might fail.

Reach out, I'm told
  Don't hold back

For you might really
  Be very much like a kite
    Never put up in the wind.

How high will it fly?
  No one knows

And they won't till it's
  Put to the test.

It starts with but a breeze and
  Then there's that tug on the
    string.

It's on the way to an
  Experience

It's afraid
  It's worried
    It might not fly

But if not for the first breeze
  That starts it to rise

It would be bound to the Earth,
  Only to die

Never to know
  How high it could fly.

Go on to the
  Experience

Be afraid
  Be worried
    It's possible you might fail.

But reach out like the kite—
  What could happen?

Well you might enjoy
  The flight.

May we be as wise as serpents and as innocent as doves as we seek to begin this new experience with single adults in churches. I can tell you, I'm really enjoying the flight.

Notes

1. *The Family Coordinator* (July 1974), p. 240.

2. Howard J. Clinebell, Jr. and Charlotte Clinebell, *The Intimate Marriage* (New York: Harper & Row, 1970). Reuel L. Howe, *The Miracle of Dialogue* (New York: Seabury Press, 1963).

6.
Handling Grief:
The Widow and the Church

Joan Salmon Campbell

I WAS THIRTY-FOUR when my world as I had known it for almost thirteen years as a wife suddenly ended. My faith in God was the sustaining and directing force as I found myself riding to the hospital, not knowing that John was already dead. I prayed aloud, "O.K. God, what are you getting me ready for now?" Before I could even leave the hospital, where John's material belongings were thrust into my hands in a green plastic trash bag, there I was—establishing priorities. What should I do first?

Even then, the church, as I had come to know and love it

JOAN SALMON CAMPBELL is a graduate of Eastman-Rochester School of Music. She is currently assistant pastor of St. Mark's United Presbyterian Church in Rockville, Md., and is a candidate for the M.Div. degree and ordination at Inter/Met Seminary (Interfaith Metropolitan Theological Education), Washington, D.C. She is president of Women of the Church of the National Capital Union Presbytery in Washington. She has sung in and directed many choirs and at present is the director of "Joan & Co."—a singing group she organized which performs music of the black religious experience.

from my parents and grandmother, was already functioning for me. I had experienced God's love for me through the love and experiences of my parents as they loved and taught me. Mother's favorite Psalm 46 all of a sudden took on crystal-clear meaning as I repeated it constantly:

> God is our refuge and strength
> a very present help in trouble (Ps. 46:1, RSV).

Many times I had witnessed mom and dad gaining this refuge and strength which seemed to buoy them up, over and through many crises. The power and essence of the church is where one's heart, mind and soul dwell. Now it was time for me to test the faith I had acclaimed and experience this refuge, as I felt God's love securely wrapped about me.

My late husband happened to be the pastor of a dynamic black congregation in Washington, D.C. As I broke the news to our five children and to John's father, I was realizing that ours was not a totally private grief, just as our life together had been a constant struggle to secure part of it in privacy. Within the hour my home seemingly swarmed with concerned people and officers of the church coming to be of assistance.

Unfortunately, they assumed for the most part that surely they needed to help Joan know what to do. I was not allowed in my own kitchen, as it was assumed that I had more important things to do, while in actuality the most important thing I wanted to do was to dispense with idleness. In their good intentions to be comforting and consoling, I found myself comforting and consoling the comforters and consolers. The deafening silence and long morbid faces were almost more depressing than John's absence. I prayed hard that God would mind my tongue and give me patience to endure my many visitors' intended kindness.

It became starkly clear to me that most of these Christians really did not understand that the death of a loved one does not

cause the living to be set with a rigor mortis of the mind, body
or spirit. It is not a time to bemoan solely the goodness of a
person whose finality will be resounded at interment. The words
came to me that had been woven in and out of my religious
heritage that "death should be a time for rejoicing for Christians." I could not then and still cannot pinpoint the author of
these words but I had to deal with their implication.

In turning to Scripture I went to 1 Corinthians 15:

> Now if Christ is preached as raised from the dead, how can
> you say that there is no resurrection of the dead? . . . We are even
> found to be misrepresenting God, because we testified that he
> raised Christ, whom he did not raise if it is true that the dead are
> not raised (1 Cor. 15:12, 15, RSV).

These words made my gut feeling rest comfortably, for I felt that
that mass of cold, hard flesh was not all that was my husband
but rather only the temporary encasement for a beautiful spirit,
steeped with a love for God and which would be ever present
with me and the children.

> For this perishable nature must put on the imperishable, and this
> mortal nature must put on immortality. . . . then shall come to
> pass the saying that is written:
> "Death is swallowed up in victory.
>   O death, where is thy victory?
>   O death, where is thy sting?" (1 Cor. 15:53–55, RSV).

The sting of death is surely the loss of a physical presence and
the grief of the living adjusting to being left behind, while the
victory for me and him is the continuing presence of his spirit
which has moved on to higher and greater presence and purpose.
Leslie D. Weatherhead states my feelings more concisely than
St. Paul:

> I am not arguing that because He [Jesus] arose from the dead,

we shall rise in the same way. Clearly we do not. He left an empty tomb. We do not. . . . evidence strongly is that we do survive and that His resurrection proves that there is another place of being in which people live.[1]

How I wished for an arena or spokesperson to help remove the shroud of mourning from those around the children and me. Even some pastors who visited carried the same almost pagan melancholy into our grief. The absence of the body at the funeral service, happy music of praise and an air of thanksgiving to God for a life beautifully lived in service to him were my determination.

Whether or not my experience is unusual, it does bring out some important points in the relationship of the widow and the church. This occasion of death brings new duties and demands to the widow—now an unwed mother-single adult. The church has a challenge and opportunity beyond dimensions of limitations to teach and support the true gospel in the world and all too often falls short of its mandate. It needs to help the widow gain a clear concept of death that accords with biblical teachings.

Here, the church should welcome the human potential movement, which can help the widow, and others, get in touch with who they are, what they think, how they feel. The movement allows them an opportunity to have a clearer perspective on where they want to go and why. A vital part of this process of discovery must be the church's proclamation of the Word. The Word that deals with the predestination of our life's purpose and the inevitable transition, at some point, into the next life.

God has set the flow of nature to help us deal with life's beginning and its termination. Morning starts the day that night ends; there is newness of life in a flower budding, but eventually it withers; leaves of trees bud, unfold fully, change colors and die. Although these things of the cosmos give us the opportunity to deal with the process of grief and change, humans unfortunately continue to squelch and bury these feelings in our "civilizing-socializing" processes. How often the church has left its true ministry to be part and parcel of establishing means to control our emotions, to deal with what appears proper as men say it should be, rather than rejoicing and celebrating the process of living and experiencing eternal life granted by Jesus. It seems that too often we fall victim to a false sense of values:

> . . . it is as though someone got into a shop in the night and altered the price labels of the things in the shop, so that the valuable things were marked low and useless things marked high. Things like obligation, service to others, a sense of duty, unselfish sacrifice, humility, these were marked low. Things like having a good time, gaining your ends, socially, sexually, materially, academically—these were marked high. . . . It's living as though there is nothing else after death and this is wrong—to say the least—mistaken. Belief in survival helps us to get our sense of values right.[2]

Though many criticize the various rites that some feel necessary to bury their dead, the church feeds the process by perpetuating traditions without adequate Christian nurture to help the rite make sense in relation to God's purpose for man. As Christians, we profess a life after death intellectually but our experiential evidence is woefully wanting. It has been pointed out that the primitive societies of the Egyptians and Tibetans seemed to express their belief in a future life better than contemporary religionists. The gesture of putting jewelry, foods, favorite articles and, in some cases, wives, into the tomb with the deceased, equipping him for the next life with what he would need, gives clear evidence of the people's belief. The church needs to help us demonstrate the faith we profess.

The absence of a loved one causes emotional and psychological grief that others cannot share. They can only offer sympathy. The way in which sympathy is offered can either loose the shackles of grief or bind them. How very important it is to continue to help the living live not only socially, financially, and with adequate food, clothing and shelter, but also by placing a Christian emphasis on that human's potential as a vital, loving, needed and contributing member of Christ's fellowship.

In summary, the single woman (widow) and the church have clear mandates to nurture each other's existence.

First the church, its preachers, and Christian educators are challenged to develop innovative and effective ways to interpret the gospel that deal with things of the spirit and life after death, and to provide opportunities that enable congregants to develop their very own theology out of their daily experiences. Meditation, Bible study, prayer, corporate worship are all viable means, but there are other ways to feed the soul. "God fulfills Himself in many ways. Anything that makes the spirit of man respond to beauty or truth or love or goodness, is enriching to the soul, and through these things he can increase his spiritual stature." [3]

Second, the congregants, who form the many parts of Christ's Body, the church, have the responsibility of knowing as professed Christians the tenets of their faith as well as the motivation and method for consoling those in grief. It is only as we begin to come to grips with death that we can fully grasp life for ourselves or for others. When I know what death is for me, then I can live life more fully.

Third, the church must sift through its stereotypes and restrictions and begin to allow the single woman (single for whatever reason) to feel a part of, rather than separate from, the fellowship of Christ. Not with pity or exceptions made, but with full recognition of her personhood as a vital, loving, needed and contributing individual.

Fourth, and most important, is the individual woman and her grounding in the faith. She must know beyond any doubt that she is a member of Christ's Body and that the church is where she is and functions best as she gives witness to God's will working in, around and through her.

Purposefully I've not emphasized the social aspects of existence for the single woman. This does not in any way imply an ostrichlike hiding from her survival needs. Task forces in cooperation with various advocacy groups can spell out and provide for those needs. Once one has the facts, a personal grounding for utilizing them is required to give confidence and direction for the single woman. The church is the one place that provides help for the shaping of total personhood. Traits, characteristics, behavior causes can be surfaced and some direction given by psychiatrists and psychologists that will help us to deal with these. But the church provides a God—the Creator—totally other and aware of our needs—who waits for us to respond to him as did Abraham, who obeyed the call to "go forth."

In these four aspects of the single woman and the church are criteria for nurturing the total church in dealing with one of life's most pressing issues—Life and Death.

> Though I am dead, grieve not for me with tears;
>   Think not of death with sorrowing and fears;
> I am so near that every tear you shed
>   Touches and tortures me, though you think me dead.
> . . . .
> But when you laugh and sing in glad delight,
>   My soul is lifted upward to the light:
> Laugh and be glad for all that Life is giving
>   And I though dead will share your joy in LIVING.
>   Source Unknown

Notes

1. Leslie D. Weatherhead, *Life Begins at Death* (Nashville: Abingdon Press, 1960).
2. Ibid.
3. Ibid.

7.
The Single-Parent Family and the Church

Robert Pinder

IT HAS BEEN ESTIMATED that nine million children under eighteen years of age in this country live with only one parent. In 1973, there were 1,453,000 single-parent families headed by fathers and 6,607,000 headed by mothers.[1] The helping professions and many churches are becoming increasingly concerned about the needs of these children and their parents. What is the profile of this significant group? What is the emotional climate of its basic units? Few answers to these questions are found in the literature on the family. Efforts in the past to examine family structure and interaction have concentrated on the complete family unit.

ROBERT PINDER is a graduate of Stetson University. He has the B.D. and Th.M. degrees from Southern Baptist Theological Seminary in Louisville, Ky., and the Th.D. degree from the University of Florida in family relations. He has pastored several churches and taught for four years at the Instituto de Rosario in Argentina. He has been associate professor of family relations at Texas Tech University in Lubbock since 1971.

Defining the Single-Parent Family

The term *single-parent* indicates that only one parent lives with the child or children while the other parent is not a participating part of the family unit. These family members experience exceptional stress. Usually these special families are created by divorce or death. However, increasing numbers are due to desertion, separation because of marital conflict, long-term separation due to vocation, and separation by institutionalization such as confinement to correctional institutions or hospitalization for mental and physical illness. Unwed mothers and single persons who adopt a child are also persons with concerns for this study.

Characteristics of the Single-Parent Family

In the single-parent family, both discipline and decision nomenon. For one thing, there is likely an underlying sense of incompleteness and frustration and a lack of fulfillment involving all of its members. The roots of these feelings are multiple. Sociocultural factors appear largely responsible for the single-parent family's constant and acute awareness of its social difference from the complete or "normal" family. The kind of feedback these families receive from others, the adjustment problems they face in conflict with the "norms" of their environment, remind them constantly of their differences. As one single parent described it: "I feel the way I imagine a person with only one leg must feel around others: conspicuous and handicapped. I am sure others feel uncomfortable with me when they are aware of my situation."

Many single parents report that they feel most "normal" during the hours of work when they are considered only as individuals without regard to family status. It is in the home and in the social sphere that the difference is frequently highlighted. Most social life for adults is planned for couples. Not only do single parents feel out of place but they feel that others perceive them as a threat to the marriage of the couples involved.

Loneliness is probably the most outstanding characteristic of single parents, regardless of the cause of their status. Emotionally, many single parents consistently miss companionship, and put this above all other needs. Specifically, they miss a partnership in the many perplexities of child-rearing, problems which could be dealt with more securely through joint responsibility. The single parent is likely to be envious of those parents who are able to turn to each other for support. But instead of the "normal" dyadic relationship of two parents, there is instead a parent-child dyad or pair. In families where there is both a mother and a father the authority of the parents is more consensual.

In the single-parent family, both discipline and decision making are more personal. The child is more likely to feel that the parent is against him when it comes to discipline, and to develop feelings of "you don't like me." The child may identify the decision-making process too much with one sex and not as a shared experience. This can be of special concern as the American family has changed from the traditional authoritarian pattern to the democratic, companionship pattern. This may cause adjustment problems in the marriage role expectations which the child carries into his future marriage.

Family life specialists are giving increasing attention to the personal functions and concerns of all of the family members, including providing for their emotional needs. Parents as well as children have needs for security, love, acceptance and fulfillment. How is the single parent to respond to his or her own needs as well as the needs of the child or children? The possibility of scapegoating thus arises—the single parent may shoulder all the blame for every problem. Unhealthy alliances is another possibility—the grouping of some family members against others. For a single-parent family, others can help to fill some of the functions, roles and affectional relationships of the missing parent. That is not to say that single parents are not able to provide children with love, affection, and emotional support. They are. And they are able even to allow the expression of negative feelings. However, the pressures on single parents make it more difficult to do this effectively.

A child generally sees himself or herself as the parents see him, influenced by the way the world sees the parents. Many of these perceptions are different for males and females. Hence some of these concepts may be distorted in the single-parent family. The self-concept and image which the single parent has and which each child has may suffer because of these experiences. The single parent has limited social ties, and will probably have less opportunity for communication and sharing with other adults. The love of the parent for the child and the child for the parent is very gratifying to the single parent but is not as supportive as adult-to-adult relationships. The single parent is generally deprived of adult relationships to meet his/her own needs.

Meeting the Needs of the Single-Parent Family

Helping Single Parents Help Themselves

Single parents can find many resources to help meet the special needs of their lives and their families; in themselves, their families, their friends, their church fellowship. Anyone who would seek to help single parents would do well to help them become aware of their own resources and develop skills needed to meet their specific responsibilities. Often the single parent needs help in learning to trust others. This may have been an area of personal need which contributed to the failure of the marriage, or perhaps they were hurt by a dominant or authoritarian spouse, or have been turned off by manipulating people they have met since becoming a single parent.

Single parents, especially those who have experienced divorce, have too often found that the church family was not able to help them in their time of frustration, loneliness and need to adjust to a new life style. An important and meaningful area of ministry is to help the church family understand the needs and experiences of these special families, and to teach them how to give understanding and support to all of the family members. I have experienced a growing awareness and concern in this area among many Christians. However, there are many pastors, church leaders and others who consistently neglect divorced persons and their families either because they lack a sympathetic, open understanding of the needs of these persons, or they are not able to translate their empathy for these persons into positive actions of acceptance and ministry.

Churches that are successful in reaching and ministering to single parents strive to build this atmosphere of acceptance and to demonstrate love in action. Acceptance and love are the primary ingredients. When single parents feel censored or rejected or are treated as second-class citizens, they drop out or make some excuse to avoid intimate fellowship. These feelings make them feel threatened, and they put up their defenses and are less than honest about their feelings and needs. As they are allowed to be themselves, to express their honest feelings, and even to work through their negative experiences they begin to make real progress in self-understanding. They are more able to let themselves be known and to open themselves to others, and they experience growth in their own personhood as well as in their relationships with others.

Though many church leaders are not trained and prepared professionally to deal with the kinds of needs these persons demonstrate, many are discovering that just being there and walking with them as caring, loving friends is the urgent need. This feeling and atmosphere cannot be faked. It has to be for real. Nothing can be substituted for genuine love and authentic people who really care. Many church workers realize they don't have the answers to all of the needs of these special families. In some cases they don't even know what the questions or problems are. However they are able to stand by and share the journey and the struggle with them. Then Christian love (agape) and fellowship (koinonia) become realized experiences and both the giver and receiver experience the community of discipleship.

The various periods of an individual's life have been defined and labeled by many behavioral scientists. One way of looking at the process of growth to maturity is that, in the usual course of development, the person can be conceived of as progressing through the stages of dependence, independence and interdependence. The stage of independence is the goal of the developmental years. During this time a young person must experience that he can survive as an independent being. He must know somehow that he has something worthwhile and valuable to offer, and that he can "make it on his own." This supposes a degree of financial independence, but vastly more important, also an emotional independence. The marriage relationship often can be a barrier to growth and maturity, with powerful pressures toward unhealthy dependence. The breakup of such a marriage may offer the opportunity for a person to achieve self-understanding and to develop an independence which can allow one to enter into a new and healthy interdependence with strength.

When marriage is a meaningful and enduring relationship, both partners feel comfortable being able to lean on the other person, knowing they will be there. It is not a lopsided relationship where one person does all the leaning against an upright and uninvolved partner. Nor is it a relationship where two partners lead parallel lives, acknowledging intermittently the existence of the other. It is not a relationship where the two people need each other so badly that they can hardly breathe apart. It is a relationship which is mutual and which very much encourages the sharing of weaknesses and strengths so that the former are lessened and the latter increased. It is this interdependent relationship that a person may experience only after he has adequately achieved his own degree of independence.

However, many marriages do not achieve this level of maturity. Often people move from their dependent state, without fully experiencing their independent state, into the interdependent state of marriage.

Recently I counseled with a young lady who had married at a young age, moving directly from her parents' home into her husband's home. After a year of marriage she became disillusioned, dissatisfied and felt cheated and unfulfilled. Through counseling, she was able to recognize that in actuality she had been in a pseudointerdependent state. She gained a lot of insight about herself. She realized her immaturity and became aware of some areas in which she needed to grow and experience expansion. She made progress through self-understanding, growth and development, and experiencing some happy interpersonal relationships. She was able to establish herself as an intact adult and move toward reconciliation with her husband and reconstruction of her marriage.

However, all too often such a recognition results both in the failure of the person to reach full growth potential and in the dissolution of the marriage. Those who work with single adults must become aware of this problem area. Single parents need to find a balance in their dependent and independent needs and to develop an ongoing interdependence in their personal relationships. In a lopsided dependent relationship, one person requires the support and enforcement of the other for an adequate sense of identity. This often results in the need of one to manipulate the other so as not to lose him and to force him to fulfill the dependent one's needs and wants.

It is important for single parents to come to an understanding and awareness of where they are in this growth process. Someone has said, "If the second marriage succeeds, then the first marriage was not a complete failure." I would hasten to say that unless divorced persons really come to some awareness of their

development in terms of dependence, independence, and interdependence in their relationships, they are not ready to consider
a second marriage, nor are they apt to be making a good adjustment in their living and relationships since the divorce.

It is particularly at this time, when the dependent aspects of
the relationship are made clear, that new opportunities for
growth and development are afforded. With this new insight,
and especially with help from others, people can change the unsatisfactory aspects of their relationships. Often during the time
of singleness, a person is afforded numerous opportunities to
catch up on interests and activities which have had to go un-
attended while many energies were being directed towards the
failing marital relationship.

The dissolution of a marriage then can be a time for enhanc-
ing maturation and creative growth, and when the unique opportunities afforded by the rediscovered single state are used to
advantage. It is most unfortunate when advantage is not taken
of these opportunities, when someone moves from an unsatisfactory marriage all too quickly into another marriage to fill any
void that might exist.

Helping Single Parents Help Their Families

Many children of divorced parents feel victimized. They are
caught up in the emotional needs of their parents, especially the
one they are living with. In addition, they are experiencing their
own emotional needs, and often frustration at school and with
their peers. The single parent tends to feel cast in the role of
accused, especially when it comes to the terms of the divorce.
The lawyer is seen as the advocate, and the other partner in the
marriage is seen as the prosecutor. The children, then, are frequently relegated to the victim spot. One ten-year-old child said
when his parents divorced, "I felt like a piece of furniture the
way they split me up between them." A younger child said,
"Nobody even asked me what I wanted. They decided without
even asking me what I felt."

When children are victimized, they feel helpless to take responsibility for their own lives and direction. In retaliation, a victimized person will begin to persecute the persecutor until the party feels like the victim. In the end, however, if this was his chosen spot, he will return to that position when establishing his own family.

Fortunately some attitudes have altered. It is not so unusual to have children living with one parent as it was ten years ago. It is not uncommon, for example, to find many children today who have no father attending the father-son banquet. Nor is it strange to find children whose mothers work and can't attend school functions.

However, it is always a negative experience when a child experiences rejection in any school, church, or community activity and is reminded that he comes from a broken family. Children of divorced parents need to know that the absence of one parent does not mean that they are unloved or loved less. They should not be allowed to feel victimized. If the parent refuses to let them get bogged down in needless self-pity, they will be encouraged to take responsibility for these negative experiences. Children need help in understanding their own feelings and working through their frustrations. They need information to help them handle difficult situations and critically analyze the real problems. Often there are alternatives the child just has not been aware existed. Many times substitute parent figures can fill the void of the absent parent.

The children of divorced parents often have difficulty accepting the fact that life will not continue like it was before, with both parents being available to attend special events. Holidays and birthdays are generally difficult times shortly after the divorce. These special times bring excitement but also pain. Many children of divorced parents share the fantasy that some day, somehow, they will get their parents back together again.

A child who is disappointed by his parents' divorce may well decide never to get close to another person again. A child whose feelings are ignored or shut off may decide to hide his feelings. A child who is overprotected or kept "the baby" may continue to seek people who care and protect him. Another child who is left by parents to handle his younger brothers and sisters long before he is able might feel he can be loved only if he takes care of others.

One way single parents can help their children unravel the hurts and disappointments of a broken family experience is to enable them to realize that they are responsible for their own behavior. They are not bound by genes to act like their father or their mother. They are not bound by their environmental experiences to repeat the life style lived before them. A good exercise for parents is to encourage their children to relate their future hopes and expectations. If they are not able to express hope for the future, or if they speak and act too much in isolation, they should be helped to separate their bad experiences of the past from their anticipation of the future and the realization of the present. This may require professional help.

The Church Ministry to the Single-Parent Family

Perhaps the best activity in any ministry to single parents is built around personal needs. The concerned helper can become more aware of the particular needs of the single parents to whom he would minister and should seek to provide realistic avenues of resources to help them meet these needs. There will be levels of needs in any group of single parents in a given church. Some are shy and need acceptance and encouragement and perhaps would be frightened by too much involvement or pressure to participate. Some may turn off the novice worker by their dress and life style. Others may have a growing self-esteem and have gotten beyond the frustrations of the initial stages of adjustment to divorce or the death of the spouse and the ensuing pressures of single parenthood. They may be ready for more involvement and need to share more responsibility for helping others. Some will be too involved in themselves, and will tend to wallow in self-pity.

Single parents are generally the best ones for reaching out to other single parents. Those who are learning to cope successfully with single parenthood can be a great help to the one who is beginning to face the realities of this new situation. "The greatest need of single parents, as I see it," a Sunday school department worker with single parents told me recently, "is to feel accepted as a person and to experience unconditional love. When divorced parents come to our department, they find people just like themselves who have experienced the same negative feelings of divorce as they themselves have experienced, namely, loneliness, bitterness, a sense of failure, frustration, and rejection. But they see these people working through these negative feelings in an atmosphere of Christian love and total acceptance."

A teacher who works with single parents in another church said to me, "We have a good fellowship in our class. Our single parents really enjoy being together. The one hour on Sunday morning was not enough so we are meeting together on Sunday nights. Once a month we have a covered-dish luncheon at the church for all single parents and their children. Activities are provided for the children. The adults mainly just visit with each other. They are learning to rebuild relationships with other males and females without the pressures of dating or other expectations of a one-to-one relationship."

Working with single parents is a very demanding ministry. Care should be given to provide fellowship and ministry for an extended time. However, one should be aware of community agencies and resources that can provide special kinds of help for single parents. Many single parents experience financial needs. Perhaps the church can provide counseling services in economic concerns. One area where churches can provide a definite ministry is in providing child care for the children.

Often the availability of single parents for employment, study, training, socializing and recreation depend on adequate care for the children.

Churches should consciously include the single-parent families in more of their programs. Communicating the grace of God is the mission of the church. There is no group that needs that ministry more than does the single-parent family.

Notes

1. *Statistical Abstract of the United States, 1974,* p. 43.

8.
Bridging the Gap: College Students and the Church

Barbara Sroka

COLLEGE STUDENTS are individual people with the common bond of education and all the experiences that come within a college or university community. They share many things: the problems of first employment, choosing majors, wrestling with papers and hourlies. But still, they are quite unlike high school students just two to six years younger. Before any discussion can take place on how the student relates to the church, we must establish who the student really is.

Out of all high school graduates 25 percent nationally attend two- or four-year schools upon graduation; 20 percent of the female and minority graduates and 30 percent of all the white males attend. The largest number come from the middle to high socioeconomic brackets, which means many of them have at

BARBARA SROKA is the assistant editor of HIS Magazine, the official magazine of Inter-Varsity Christian Fellowship U.S.A. and Canada, a position which allows her to be in frequent contact with college students. She is a graduate of the University of Illinois with a B.Sc. degree in journalism.

least one parent who is a college graduate. Of those students who begin their education, only two-thirds to three-quarters will finish.

The largest demographic factor affecting the church in regard to college attendance is geographic location. Because people of the same standard of living settle in the same areas, the bulk of college students in any one college or geographic area will come from the areas of middle or high socioeconomic concentration. For instance, the school system in Downers Grove, Illinois, one of the affluent western suburbs of Chicago, sends approximately 60 percent of its high school graduates to two- or four-year colleges or universities. That's more than twice the national average. A pastor in Downers Grove, then, will probably be dealing with many more students on the average than other pastors across the nation during the summer. A college program for one student would be considered ridiculous. Lack of a college program if there are eighty students in the congregation would be equally ridiculous. If the church is near a university campus, contact with college students will be year-round.

Different geographic areas will produce students with differing needs. The students' expectations and difficulties will vary. Those from the high economic areas will most likely be concerned with their own lives in an achievement and self-fulfillment oriented way. They'll also have concerns for the poor, the environment, bad government, and where the United States is heading as a country.

The main concern of students who are part of minority groups is for their own future in an institutionally racist society. All their concerns are tempered by the overwhelming problem of racism. They'll also have difficulties adjusting to a white university community whose social structure gears itself toward in the white middle class—where the money lies.

As another minority group transcending all geographic areas, nontraditionalist women experience unique frustrations. The church often does not acknowledge their needs and concerns as valid. These women feel that the church has placed sexism on the level of principle. If I were asked who is most turned off by the church today, I would have to say this group of students. They're concerned with institutional sexism and how that affects their futures as professionals.

Campus experiences of all these students will vary, but the greatest difference exists between Christian colleges and secular collges and universities. The environments are so different that their students often have completely different needs.

I have been fortunate enough to work with both Youth for Christ (YFC) staff and Inter-Varsity Christian Fellowship (IVCF) staff in the last two years. Youth for Christ staff come largely from Christian colleges while Inter-Varsity staff come from secular campuses. Why do these graduates divide so neatly between organizations like this? One reason is that it's natural for a family to stick together. Because Inter-Varsity graduates remember the help they got from IVCF in their undergraduate careers, they work for IVCF. Likewise, Youth for Christ graduates remember the help of YFC in their high school days and join their staff team.

A Christian college provides students with a sheltered environment in which they don't have to deal with the multitudes of non-Christians. Students in these schools, however, know more about the Bible, doctrine, church history, and Christian literature. Many of them come from Christian homes or are missionaries' children. Often there is a greater concern among them for overseas missions than for domestic missions. This is due, I believe, not only to home environment, but also to college courses on missions, Foreign Missions Fellowship, and the Urbana missionary convention.

The Christian college student, lacking the stimulation of dealing with non-Christians daily, is often more complacent about the Christian faith. The isolationism of the Christian campus can also breed cynicism about the church and most Christian institutions. The day-to-day contact among Christians leads to a

greater awareness of the faults in the church or college. The
reformers of church institutions come largely from Christian
schools. The better percentage of Richard Quebedeaux's
"Young Evangelicals" [1] are Christian college graduates. The
founding editors of *The Post American* attended Trinity
Evangelical Divinity School in Deerfield, Illinois.

There exists what I tend to call the "Christian school myth,"
which states that by sending high school students to Christian
colleges, you'll put them in an environment where they won't
"lose their faith." That isn't necessarily so. The Christian college is not designed to be a surrogate parent, looking after the
"kids" and seeing that Suzie brushes her teeth. It is an institution of higher learning and can be just as impersonal as a state
university which, contrary to rumor, is usually not completely
impersonal.

My experience bears this out. Out of all the graduating se-
niors in my YFC group, I was the only one who didn't go to a
Christian school. Today, I am one of two in Christian work,
another married a Christian and settled into family life, and the
other three have "lost their faith." By "lost their faith" I mean
that for all practical purposes they do not acknowledge that
Jesus Christ is important in their lives, even to the point of
denial. My experience is probably extreme and not reflective of
what happens generally. But this can and has happened, and we
should all be aware of it. I don't believe that the Christian
schools caused these people to fall from actively following the
Lord. But no matter how diligent Christian parents or Christian
schools are, a person predisposed to leaving the faith will likely
do so.

The major problem Christian students are faced with, which
most of them are aware of, is being challenged in their own faith.
The Christian college student has usually transferred from one
Christian environment to another. He has yet to be challenged
with living continually in a worldly, often hostile, atmosphere.
This means he has not had a chance to make his faith his own.

He has not experienced isolation from other Christian believers in his living quarters where faith is most severely tested in the college atmosphere. And faith untested is immature. The church flourishes under persecution.

A secular campus, quite contrary to what is commonly thought, can be very friendly and warm. Whether large or small, it can be compared to a small town. A camaraderie exists, a spirit of "we're all in this together." There's a combined and sometimes contrary optimism and pessimism. The students know they are the minds and creative thought of the future, yet they're well aware of the shape of society today. The secular college or university community allows for great growth in the students who live there, even for evangelical students who want to grow closer to the Lord. Peer influence which was so strong in high school lessens. Individuality replaces conformity in importance. Students compete with each other for grades as a matter of survival.

Christian students on a secular campus don't usually have a formal biblical education. They also learn within the first week of the school year that they are in the minority on campus. So, without saying a word, Christian students will stand out. The positive attitudes Christians have tell who they are. The life style speaks. In the November 1975 issue of *HIS*, IVCF campus staff member Terrell Smith tells of his first day on campus:

"As I was unpacking my books, including my Bible, a great opportunity [for witness] appeared. I laid my Bible down on my desk. My new roommate saw that and said, 'You're not some kind of a Christian, are you?' Actually he used words a little stronger than that. I wasn't sure how to answer because of the words he used. But just because I took my Bible out and laid it there I was visible."

A first day like Terrell's is usually enough to drive any Christian to the nearest Bible study he or she can find. There are some casualties. But there are many responses like Terrell's, too. Sunday morning church, prayer and praise meetings, Bible studies and prayer partners are very popular. They are the fuel to keep going.

The basic difference between Christian college students and Christian students on secular campuses is that those on secular campuses have had their faith questioned and put to the test. Knowing what and why they believe is necessary for survival, not merely to pass an exam. There's nothing like the challenge presented by walking into Philosophy 110, World Religions, on the first day, hearing the lecturer say he's a Christian and then add, "Although I don't believe that garbage about Jesus being God and I think the resurrection is a hoax."

A good percentage, well over 50 percent in my college experience, of the Christians at secular schools were converted while on campus. They come from all kinds of backgrounds: Christian homes, wealthy homes, radical homes, humanist homes, agnostic homes. Sometimes, non-Christian parents react very negatively to their child's conversion. Walter Hearn, in the June 1975 issue of *HIS*, relates the reaction of one set of parents whose daughter, Ann, was converted her freshman year.

"She had written to her parents in Washington, D.C., that she'd become a Christian. They panicked, sure that she'd fallen in with a bunch of fanatics. Her father had called as soon as he'd read her letter: either get herself straightened out, or they'd come take her out of school." She managed to calm her parents, however, and remained in school.

Most of these converted students don't have a home church. Their spiritual lives are nurtured at school through the non-denominational Christian organizations on campus (Campus Crusade for Christ, The Navigators, Inter-Varsity Christian Fellowship), the denominational foundations (Baptist Student Union, Lutheran Student Foundation, Newman Center, etc.), the local evangelical church, or a combination of the above.

The myth of the Christian on the secular campus is the converse of the myth of the Christian college. A Christian student will not necessarily lose his or her faith. There's no guarantee. However, from a pastor's point of view, it sometimes looks as if the lambs are being sent to a spiritual slaughter. And sometimes it's hard to judge when one sees students only on vacations.

Misconceptions about Students

Because there are a number of common misunderstandings of student personalities, I'd like to analyze some of them. Like all generalizations, however, they don't always hold.

All students are lazy—like electricity, students always seek the path of least resistance. This depends on the individual. But if a student is getting good grades, chances are he's less lazy than might be suspected. What he or she does on holidays (sleeping in till ten every morning) doesn't necessarily reflect school behavior. In fact, a great many are overworked. Today, school costs are so high that many students work not only in summers, but during the academic year. Medical statistics (from the University of Illinois health center, Urbana-Champaign) show that up to 90 percent of all students will have contracted mononucleosis at some time during their undergraduate careers. Mono, falsely labeled "kissing disease," strikes those who are fatigued and in situations of great stress.

In addition in some fields of study, practical experience is as important as academic study and a degree. Virtually all fine arts majors, psychology majors, and journalism majors must do extracurricular work if they intend ever to get into their chosen professions. Their involvement usually averages a commitment of fifteen to twenty hours per week and can be as much as eighty to one hundred hours a week outside of class and study time.

Students like to party, party, party. True, the party is a major form of entertainment, but it isn't daily, and most often, isn't even weekly. Parties and pranks will always be a part of student life, and I think that's good. Some pranks don't even take very long. My sister tells me that it took fifteen girls only thirty minutes to build a snow turkey on the Sigma Chi front lawn last January. Most students, at least those who graduate, spend the bulk of their time studying.

Students are idealistic. This implies that students don't face up to reality and that truth must be watered down or kept from them. Of all the myths, this is the least founded. In fact, operating on this myth is a sure way to lose the interest of any college student.

Students rebel against all authority. This depends on the individual. But often, it's hard to discern between rebellion and true questioning. The student is often not rebellious, but is rather trying to figure things out for himself.

Students fall easily for poor doctrine. Not really. This again depends on the individual. In every age group there are those prone to accepting things without question. Remember, both Eve and Adam never attended college.

This is the first time in their lives they've begun to question. No! This is just the first time they've boldly expressed themselves. The process began years ago, and therefore the questions are deeply rooted. Superficial, well-worn answers will be inadequate.

Students will be swayed by university teaching, especially by humanists and evolutionists. The questions humanists and evolutionists present will make the Christian student think. But, most Christian students are stronger each time their faith is put to the test and the truth wins out.

Students can't make intelligent decisions. They're blown about in the wind. It's true, many can't. But many can. Then again, there are many people of *all* ages who can't make decisions.

There's another attitude toward students that's hard to put the finger on. The feeling that there's something less responsive, less aggressive, less directive, less creative—just less of everything adult—about a student. There is a behavior, regardless of intellect or talent, that just makes adults nervous about trusting students with their own growth. I call it the "student posture."

Students have adopted a posture that they automatically fall into in the presence of anyone remotely associated with authority. It's a submissive posture that assumes that the authority figure is in the teaching position and *expects* to be in the teaching position, and if the student dares cross this authority, there will be some negative response from that authority. The posture assumes that the authority figure will want to lead anything he or she is involved in. It's a posture of participating within a group but not becoming an authority figure.

The student posture is a natural for all students. Most of their lives have been spent under the rule of parents, who spent virtually all of those eighteen to twenty years developing that child under authority. Authority and peer interaction were the two most common interpersonal relationships a child had, with authority being the more significant (whether parents believe it or not). College and university life continues the authority structure. The student is under the influence of instructors, professors, and graduate students (all authorities) who will determine for a large part their success as students. They merely adjust their posture from relating to parents to coping with instructors. It's a social system.

Every student, no matter how rebellious, does this. At an Inter-Varsity camp for college students recently, I was impressed by the main goal of the staff: to make the campers shed some of their submissive student skin in order to lead their own spiritual lives aggressively and become leaders of other students.

Since the student will fall into this submissive posture so easily, it's very easy to accept it as the real picture and not try to draw the student out of it. But one needs to remember that there is more to this seemingly dependent student. The student posture is not the person.

Student Needs

Students have many needs. Some apply to all students, others are peculiar to the different subgroups of students. The basic need is for students to break away in order to look at themselves and all they've been involved in their entire lives, and then to piece together a life for themselves. In doing this, of course, they will make mistakes, they will have difficulties, and will experience tragedies. Students are people.

Students need their own identity. Developing personhood is a critical issue at this time of life. There's nothing quite like your curriculum adviser calling you into his or her office at the beginning of your sophomore year and demanding that you make your decision on your major by spring. The nineteen-year-old is asked to make a decision that could affect the course of a lifetime. Identity is intertwined with the whole problem of selection of a major. Questions like "What do I like to do? Where are my talents?" aren't easily answered.

Some may think that the search for identity is just a middle-class luxury, implanted in students' minds by the 60s generation. These people see identity as something peripheral to life, while the important things are developing responsibility, gaining confidence, serving God selflessly, and growing in personal discipleship. Essentially, they believe that all the identity any Christian needs is to be identified with Christ. Christian students will not deny the importance of these aims. But they will insist on the search for identity in order to find who they are uniquely in Christ and how their particular characteristics, gifts and talents can be used in the Body of Christ.

Identity is a tool for living. Knowing yourself helps in formulating goals and accepting limitations. One of the most obvious areas in which identity is important is marriage. Knowing limitations, strengths, abilities and concerns helps deduce a person's needs in a marriage partner.

Students need to be recognized as adults. In loco parentis (in place of parents) doesn't hold any more, except at the most conservative Christian schools. But even at these conservative schools, students are essentially governing their own lives, because no one is there to force them to their primary responsibility: study. They are responsible for their success in school and therefore essentially responsible for themselves. Stereos, rock concerts and water fights shouldn't obscure this point. The same student who participates in these activities writes term papers on "White Rat Behavior: The Effects of Overcrowding" or edits the university newspaper (which may have a staff of 120 editors and reporters).

The challenges presented by the college or university are many. The environment is not like high school where the administration tries its best to see that no one is left behind. The college student must compete from his first eight o'clock class on a September morning until those diplomas are presented.

One youth pastor I interviewed admitted that the church often insults students by not recognizing their maturity. Churches don't realize what students are capable of, what they contend with on a college campus, or what their concerns are. And the students are hurt when they aren't taken seriously. An informal survey of IVCF staff showed that the primary concern of Christian students today is guidance. "What shall I do with my life? Should I go into full-time Christian work?" Their secondary concern is for unsaved family and friends. These are adult concerns.

Students need to be learners not students. The difference between being a student and a learner is the difference between passively being taught and aggressively digging in and studying the Word on one's own. Preaching to students should be left in the pulpit.

Students need to be listened to. The younger the person the greater the temptation to lecture them. But the opposite is what they need—someone who will use all their good listening techniques.

They need to be encouraged in creative thought about the church. It may not be true, but the student thinks that both pastor and parishioners don't want anyone to change what they've established. And therefore it's no use for them to get involved in the church or to express their views on what needs to be done.

They need all of the above dealt with in honesty. The truth must always win out. Skirting an issue, dealing superficially, delivering unexplained ultimatums, insincere motives, condescending attitudes, sugar-coating reality, and denying faults are sure ways to lose college students. They demand honesty, something entertainer Johnny Carson realized. "You have to deal with college students honestly," he has said. "You must be yourself or they'll walk out on you."

Students won't get up and walk out on the church; they'll just stop coming. A student at Gordon College told me a few weeks ago that he's stopped going to his home church because of the infighting. He said attendance for him was "a burden not a help."

Relating to Students

How does the local church, nestled in some area far from the college campus, relate to these students, these foreigners?

"Relating" and "meeting needs" are not altogether accurate ways to describe how the church will be of most aid to college students. No life style, the church's or the students', needs to be sacrificed in an attempt to relate. The family structure of the church and the independent life style of the student don't have to be antagonistic. In fact, the church should look upon the meeting of these two life styles as an opportunity.

The student has learned much from the college atmosphere. The church has the opportunity to show the student how what he or she has learned can have a practical outlet. The student often feels as if he's living in a world of theory, without tangible substance. That doesn't mean the university world is any less real. It is real. There's just not as much chance to use what's learned.

As I've mentioned, a good number of Christian college students on secular campuses were converted after they began college. They don't have a home church, and they might lack Christian fellowship for the summer if they are the only Chris-

tian in the family. The local church can provide needed support
for these students, but finding them might be difficult. These
students often have no idea what churches in their hometowns
will be able to or even want to meet their needs. The national
offices of the three large campus organizations (IVCF, CCC,
and the Navigators) can supply the names and addresses of the
staff of these organizations in the church's locality. A letter sent
in early spring, giving church location, and offering fellowship
to students who will be in the area during the summer will almost surely be relayed to both staff and students.

As members of the Body of Christ, we are responsible for
one another—for all ages, occupations, and life styles. But let's
face facts. We're often rejected by each other and don't feel we
can support each other's life styles. Sometimes we don't want
to or aren't capable of accepting the responsibility. College
students and home churches are equally guilty of this rejection.

There are several reasons why students don't attend local
churches. The biggest one is that the church isn't meeting their
needs. That doesn't mean the student is ignoring his own spiritual needs. Many will be involved in weekly Bible studies with
other students in their home area from their school. Students will
go a long way for fellowship. For two summers, I traveled over
twenty miles to attend a weekly Bible study.

Students are also in a transition period of life. They're changing. They might change in a way that makes church attendance
difficult for them. This may be a temporary phase; it may be
permanent. But it's important to remember that they haven't
dropped their faith, just the church.

Some say that they don't see church as important to their
lives. What they're actually saying is that the family structure
of the church isn't important to them. They have other needs
now.

Students may claim that the home church is too dull. There's
a lot behind a statement like that, and no pastor should ignore
the charge. Rather he should ask the student in for a private

talk and find out his reasons for such a statement. Some will be valid and need to be considered carefully; others will not.

Still, with all said and done, I think it's important for all pastors and church members to realize that no matter what a church does or how much concern it has, some students will not respond through no fault of theirs or of the church.

How can a church affect the lives of its student members and attenders? A body of believers should be aware that its children will one day make a choice of whether to stay within a particular denomination or a church. They'll be making decisions and one of those decisions will concern whether church is important to them or not. There are ways to help make fellowship within a particular church important no matter what the age. The college student poses a different kind of problem because they're mostly seen only during the summer months.

Each member of the church must take some of the responsibility for its college students in the way of personal contact. The pastor or youth pastor can't do it all. By personal contact, I mean being involved in the students' lives. This is true whether they are Christian college students or Christian students on secular campuses, and most of the following suggestions are appropriate for both groups.

The first weeks on a secular campus are more difficult than those on a Christian college campus in terms of lacking contact with other Christians. It can be a great help to any secular school freshman if someone notifies the local staff member of Inter-Varsity or Campus Crusade or the Navigators or the denominational foundations, depending on the student's choice, at that school and gives them the student's name. Or, if there are older college students from the same congregation on that campus the church should try to get them together beforehand so they can work something out for fall.

One IVCF staff member has suggested that churches commission Christian students when they leave for secular campuses much as a missionary is commissioned. IVCF, Campus Crusade for Christ, and the Navigators all consider the students involved in their groups as missionaries to the campus. The IVCF three-pronged purpose is *evangelism,* discipleship, and missions.

Pastors should also feel free to ask students to write letters to the entire congregation. And the congregation should reciprocate on an individual level. One IVCF staff wife talks freely and thankfully about her home church and their faithful support throughout her school years. It's not enough just to send "official" mailings. If churches expect students to be faithful in returning to them during the summer months, they must be faithful to the students.

The ways of keeping in contact are as many as anyone can think up. Here are some.

Send them books that are currently significant to you. These should not be material you think they ought to read. This must be a sharing exercise, not a teaching one. A pastor might consider sending a book related to the subjects of the sermons planned for the months the student is away, to help keep the student growing with the congregation.

Gather news from each student, and compile and circulate a newsletter among them. Also make sure each church member receives a copy.

Buy each student a gift subscription to *HIS* Magazine. My prejudice may be showing here. But *HIS* is the only magazine in the United States for Christian students. We promise to land one in student mailboxes every month, from October through June. There are discounted rates for subscribing in large numbers.

InterVarsity Press will send you a catalog and Press-o-matic brochures free. IVP is the only book publisher specifically publishing for students. Press-o-matic is the InterVarsity Press book club, and through it all IVP titles can be purchased at 20 percent off, with no obligation to purchase a certain amount. Many denominational publishing houses have books aimed at the student market.

Some churches sponsor retreats at Christmas break. If your church does, make sure it is high on content and make the "frosting" a fun time. Or if a retreat is impossible, consider having a student dinner during Christmas break.

Encourage members of the congregation to phone the students (once a semester from every church member means a lot of phone calls) to chat socially.

Send goodies. Homemade cookies, fudge, brownies, candies, toasted nuts are real treats to supplement dorm food.

By using the imagination, personal contact can be maintained. It's very difficult for any human being to turn his back on those who show that they care.

They've come back for the summer, now what do you do with them? I want to reaffirm: College students are not *kids,* they want meat not milk. *HIS* Magazine received a lengthy letter from a Christian girl, brought up in the church, who was somewhat bitter about her experience.

FUN, FOOD and FROLIC is the motto in some churches. The meetings consist of a lot of choruses vigorously sung, testimonies, and Bible studies on the journeys of Paul. None of this is wrong. Far from it. It is all very necessary in the life of a Christian young person. However, I do believe that it is all basically a superficial treatment of the Christian faith and of life in general. It is fairly easy to fall into the correct phraseology, the correct type of smile and the correct tone of voice that are accepted in this kind of atmosphere. It is easy to be "fake" and I believe that this is where the problem lies.

What she calls "fake," I call the "student posture." Her whole letter stressed the need for content and depth in Christian programs for young adults. (I don't believe any church tries to keep its young people from being prepared. In fact, I know there is often great effort put forth in that direction.)

Good summer programs have similar characteristics. They are at a time convenient to most students. Summer jobs frequently have weird hours, so it might be difficult to accommodate everyone.

Good summer programs "shoot high" by dealing in depth with student needs and concerns. And they're honest and open. As an example, Jim McCue of Christ Church, Oak Brook, Illinois, has prepared a three-pronged approach for their summer program: the Bible, the Body of Christ, and the world. Emphasis is placed on good biblical teaching and learning, developing sound relationships within the Body of Christ, and developing the skills to communicate faith to others. Students meet twice weekly, Sunday night for study and fellowship and Monday night for outreach.

No matter what method a church uses, all programs should emphasize developing leadership qualities and discipleship.

Up until now, Sunday school material hasn't been written for college students or the young working person. After high school, a person moves into an adult study, even though the needs of this age group are so radically different from other adults.

To fill this need, David C. Cook Publishing Co. introduced a new curriculum in December 1975 called LifeStyle. It deals with the problems and needs outlined in this essay. In the introduction to the study guide, curriculum editor Denny Rydberg wrote:

> The LifeStyle experience of *learning together* is almost the perfect opposite of the courses (you've probably taken more than one of them) where you sat at the feet of a Ph.D. who poured information into your cranium à la potatoes into a sack. Fifty minutes four times a week—he talked, you listened and scribbled (or daydreamed, or slept). He was the authority, you were the humble listener.
>
> In contrast, a LifeStyle course has no lectures, no gurus, and hopefully, no boredom. It is a group of Christians and maybe-Christians coming together to question, to wonder, to ask, to seek, to knock . . . and to find the door being opened as together they explore God's truth.

Together . . . exploring God's truth . . . isn't that what
the church is all about?

Notes

1. Richard Quebedeaux, *The Young Evangelicals* (New York:
Harper & Row, 1974).

9.
The Church Cares for the College Student

Rich Berry

ALMOST TWO THOUSAND years have passed since Jesus declared to Peter and the disciples that he would build his church and the gates of hell could not prevail against it. God has made it very clear through the centuries that the church is his instrument for communicating the gospel to the world. Despite persecution and major efforts to destroy this institution, the church is still alive and kicking.

In order for the church to be effective in this generation, it must make inroads into every segment of our society. The early church did this by reaching both the common people and the intellectuals, the rich and the poor. Peter and John were said to be "unlearned and ignorant men" (Acts 4:13, KJV), but God used them in the lives of many including those in high positions of authority (Acts 10:25).

RICH BERRY is area director for the Navigators in Atlanta, Georgia, where he works with collegiates and couples in the black community. He became acquainted with the Navigators during his four years in the Air Force. Mr. Berry is married and has one son.

The college campus is said to be among the most challenging mission fields in the world. Nearly 50 percent of the population of the United States is in college. Unfortunately Christianity has little credibility among these millions of young people. One reason for its ineffectiveness is that the Christian community has placed too much emphasis on the spiritual needs of a man with little or no attention to his mental and social development. Students have viewed this as an inconsistency and have labeled Christians as being hypocritical and on a spiritual high, unaware of the realities of life. This dichotomy has driven many students to agree with Karl Marx, who referred to religion as "the opium of the people." Perhaps the college community has also failed in the development of the total individual by majoring on the social and mental needs at the expense of the spiritual. This misemphasis on both sides has created a chasm between the two, made rivals of collegiates and the church rather than interdependent relatives.

Reaching the College Student

The Rational Thinker

In order to evangelize and disciple college students effectively, one must first be aware of how they think. Collegiates are trained to analyze, criticize, and make logical assumptions. Traditionally, the church has avoided intellectualizing biblical truths, merely accepting them by faith without question. Consequently the student community has rejected the church as being anti-intellectual. This is not to say, however, that every biblical truth can be rationalized, but it is a plea supporting the use of Christian apologetics. During Paul's early ministry, there is clear indication that he appealed to the intellect of the Jews in the synagogue (See Acts 9:22). Churchmen must be sensitive to the proper use of apologetics as it relates to the college student.

Majoring on the Minors

Much of what is preached to non-Christian students is often inappropriate and applicable only to Christians in a discipleship class. It seems almost forgotten that an unbeliever has no real power to correct sin in his life except through the Holy Spirit. Permissive sex, length of hair, smoking, drinking and dress are often made the object of the worldliness sermon. Consequently the collegiate feels condemned and views Christ as a kill-joy. Christianity to him becomes repressive, representing a long list of "dos and don'ts." The collegiate's morality is a minor issue when viewed with respect to his lostness and separation from God. In the Sermon on the Mount Jesus placed far more emphasis on worldly *thinking* and attitudes than on actions (Matt. 5:28). What Jesus considered major issues, such as one's life style and character, the church relegates to minor ones and vice versa. Another drawback as a result of this misemphasis is that many church people, perhaps unknowingly, view worldliness with a cultural bias. Judging worldliness from a cultural position is not new. The early church suffered from the same problem. One such case may be seen in Romans 14. The Jewish Christians expected the gentile converts to take on their cultural traditions in order to grow and be "fully" Christian, but Paul rebuked that attitude and challenged them not to judge another man by his outward actions (Rom. 14:1–12).

Understanding the Great Commission

Probably the most talked about and yet most misunderstood command in the New Testament is the Great Commission. Prior to his ascension, Jesus told his disciples to "go . . . and make disciples of all nations" (Matt. 28:18, RSV). Historically, the church has made an unsuccessful attempt to practice this commission as it was originally intended. The emphasis has been on *go*. Go out for God, go across the seas, go to Africa (the most difficult place to serve. This is a gross misunderstanding of Christ's commission.

Actually the word translated *go* is a participle in the Greek, and therefore "could be literally translated as *going,* or, as you are going." [1] The emphasis is on making disciples, wherever the church is or goes. The church is always to *be* in the process of making disciples; it is not to be waiting to go off somewhere.

What does this have to do with college students? Just this. The Christian community must view the campus not as some place to visit and do evangelism and then leave, to come back to the safety of the sanctuary. Students, particularly those away from home, are looking for relationships not affiliations. One cannot develop a meaningful relationship in a one-shot presentation of the gospel. Students feel that Christians are out to save their souls with little concern for their personal lives.

The issue here is friendship evangelism. The process by which a person's friendship and trust is won and the life style exhibited become as much the message as what is said. The amount of partying on the average college campus is indicative of the need collegiates have for meaningful interpersonal relationships. The Christian can easily meet this need by becoming friends with a college student.

Don't Crowd the Right

The large superchurches of our nation have memberships that generally represent white middle-class America. In almost every case the evangelistic outreaches of these successful churches say to the rest of the world, "Come get a dose of salvation and be like us." Their programs are often out of touch with that segment of the student community who have already rejected the status quo and have aligned themselves with those on the Left who are trying to change the system. Christians must stop crowding out the Right, having programs that appeal primarily to those on the Right. Historically, the church has aligned itself with the "God and Country" ideal. In America, it has not separated itself from the oppressive system which the majority of college students are out to change. Presently, social involvement on the part of the evangelical church is still low on the list of priorities. By such lack of action on the behalf of equality and justice, the church has failed to communicate the idea that Jesus was neither communist nor capitalist, on the Right or on the Left, but acting in behalf of all peoples, all races, all political persuasions.

The church is not on the cutting edge of justice and positive change in our society because it is not addressing itself to controversial questions people are asking. A graduating collegiate from a religious college was counseled by his advisor, "Any Christian movement that creates too much controversy is not of God." This counselor, along with many others, has missed the purpose for which Christ died. Christ died to radically change men's lives. Whenever men are filled with the Spirit of God they will be controversial. Peter and John and Paul were willing to be beaten and killed for the controversial cause of Christ. Had they decided not to be on the cutting edge, the church might not be where it is today.

Many student activists are sincere in their efforts to change the world. They have zeal but without knowledge or clear direction. One cannot argue with their diagnosis of the problems ailing our society. They have done their homework. The issue is how can this radical student understand that change, true change, can come about only when people change, and only Christ can change people. Students who are involved with an activist movement are hard to reach and require major sacrifices on the part of the congregation which has decided to take on such a venture.

If a campus has a large body of dissidents, then what Paul says applies to the nearby congregation or congregations: "I am made all things to all men, that I might by all means save some" (1 Cor. 9:22, KJV). Christians must answer the questions those students are asking by trying to view their perplexities from the students' point of reference. Reaching the radical Left calls for more than just changing sermons and giving out new tracts. It means a new way of thinking, new attitudes and a willingness to create a "Third Way." "In this practice of the Third Way, Christians together should be seen as a reconciling community, healing the divisions, de-fusing hostility, bridging communication gaps." [2]

Training and Discipling the College Student

Dawson Trotman, founder of the Navigators, discovered early in his ministry that to have the most effective ministry, he could not merely win someone to Christ, turn him over to God, and go about his business of preaching. The emphasis that the Navigators place on discipleship grew out of Trotman's realization that God has called the church to major on two areas, one being evangelism and the other discipleship.

In order for a campus ministry to grow and last, the process of training and discipling must be all-important. Many churches are involved in training and discipleship but are falling short of Jesus' example. The elements of character development and commitment to the absolute lordship of Christ must be the goals. The extent of discipleship in the minds of many is to take a convert through a two-month course and teach him to share his faith. But that's not enough.

College students are available and are waiting to be molded. Discipleship training conserves the fruit of evangelism. The need to disciple stands out as the greatest need after conversion. Jesus was concerned about the one sheep out of the hundred that was lost. Traditional Christian ministries have gone so far to the other extreme that most are satisfied with the one staying and the ninety-nine leaving. Jesus promised that one's fruit would remain (John 15:16). When one understands and practices Christ's methods of discipling, the truth of this promise will be evident.

Not Just a Decision

The conversion experience is more than a resolution. It is a completely new way of living. What begins with a decision should continue to grow into a life filled with the Spirit and conformed to the image of Christ.

The evangelical community has virtually reduced discipleship to a mere decision. Sharing a five-minute gospel outline, leading a person to Christ and then sending a follow-up letter is a sorry excuse for *fulfilling* the Great Commission. Many evangelistic programs merely offer statistics on how many came forward and the number baptized. With so little emphasis on the number of those continuing on in the Christian life, it is no wonder that those collegiates who have made decisions soon fall away.

The importance of commitment for the young Christian is magnified when one views the campus environment with all its temptations. Sex and drugs, Eastern religions and pagan cults are always bartering for his time and thoughts. Many have been lost to this Satan-dominated environment.

The church must be willing to be what the Apostle Paul was —"a nursing mother cherishing her own children" (1 Thess. 2:7, Weymouth)—to the young collegiate.

Turn Up Your Light

The changes that take place in the life of the disciple are not primarily a result of preaching, but of what he sees in the life of the disciple-maker. Principles of life are more caught than taught. If after a student comes to Christ he is not able to identify with the life of the spiritual parent, his is quite likely to be an abortive attempt at the Christian life for lack of having proper images to follow.

In his letter to the Philippians, Paul insisted that they follow his example (Phil. 4:9). Jesus, in his Sermon on the Mount, brings out the importance of being an example. "Let your light so shine before men, that they may see your good works, and glorify your Father which is in heaven" (Matt. 5:16, KJV). With the barrage of hypocrisy and the diminishing of morality in campus life, the student is particularly atuned to the life of the disciple-maker. Young Christians are also anxious to hear about the "not so glamorous" stories—the failures. Christians tend to promote the "all is well," "heavenly sunshine" type of image. Students, like all of us, go through struggles which they think no one else has. When they hear that a Christian leader also faces the same temptations, it makes a great impression and communicates the realities of living for Christ. Total honesty on the part of the disciple-maker is a must.

Paul said to Timothy, "Now you have observed my teaching, my conduct, my aim in life, my faith, my patience, my love, my steadfastness, my persecutions, my sufferings," (2 Tim. 3:10–11, RSV).

Where There Is No Vision

Motivating students to grow in discipleship is accomplished when a church has an objective that is *understood* and *biblically based*.

Most churches have lost the primary objectives of evangelism and discipleship, with the result that the pastor tries to orchestrate a disarray of programs and organizations, for which money must be raised to maintain them. When the church lacks clear, biblical objectives, the average student has little motivation to become involved. "Where there is no vision, the people are unrestrained" (Prov. 29:18, NAS).

The student community is drilled with the importance of being organized and goal-centered. The local congregation must provide meaningful involvement for ambitious students or they will seek fulfillment elsewhere.

On the other extreme is the church that is overly organized and has lost its sensitivity for the individual. God has not inspired the American Management Association to write another epistle to the New Testament. Sensitivity to the Holy Spirit is essential for keeping a balance.

In addition to clear vision, a student will be motivated when he is given some sort of responsibility. IBM has discovered this great universal principle, applied it to its corporation, and is making millions.

The student must have growing room in the church or he will channel his energies into other groups, organizations and social causes outside the church that are bidding for his life. The Sunday school program is an excellent outlet for students in educational fields of training. Creative church planning can utilize students' gifts and abilities in a way that will be an asset both to the collegiate and to the church.

The student must also be made aware of the mission boards offering professional missionary opportunity. In addition to local church work, this could provide the student with an overseas tour wherein he can utilize his training.

A Home Away from Home

Numerous studies have been produced in recent years on the importance of the family and its effect on developing mature young people who will have an effect on changing the society. Children don't come into the world with a self-image. It is almost exclusively a result of home life.

The high degree of frustration and depression on the part of Christian college students can often be traced back to their home life. The biggest need among these college students is one of reaffirmation, to believe in spite of what they were taught at home that they are amazingly and wonderfully made by God (Ps. 139:14). Although rebellion against parents is never justified, one can sympathize with many young people who come from homes where parents were always on their backs.

The church worker must be keenly aware that he may be able to make a contribution to this young collegiate that will affect his entire life. As was mentioned earlier, to be a disciple means to identify with the life of the disciple-maker. There is

no greater example than that of one's home life. The Apostle
Paul said that if ever you want to know what the relationship
between Christ and the church should be, check with the Christian home (Eph. 5:22–30). The home, therefore, provides an
excellent model for the young disciple to see Christianity in action. If the student has had a bad family background, identification with a Christian home will also provide him with a
firsthand course on how, when he gets married, his family
should operate.

The temptation for any Christian worker is to go home to his
family and leave his ministry on campus, or at church, and
thereby miss a great opportunity to minister to his disciples.

In their disciple-making process, the Navigators have taken
advantage of opening their homes to selected leadership workers to train and expose them to "where the action really is." The
student has an opportunity to identify with the disciple-maker
as he really is. Anyone with a family knows he can fake Christian character on the platform but everything comes out at
home. This type of exposure does wonders for developing the
young disciple. If he is from a broken or non-Christian home,
he gets a firsthand account of how Christians live where it counts
the most. This type of in-home training in no way suggests
sacrificing the sanctity of the home for a service environment.
The emphasis here is placed on a maturing young person becoming a part of your family for a period of time. A second
home for a growing Christian student cannot substitute for all
that he should have received at home growing up, but it can
help in many ways to provide a practical example that God can
use in filling the gap.

Solomon said, "Train up a child in the way he should go,
and even when he is old he will not depart from it" (Prov.
22:6, ASV). The Christian community can perform a miracle
in a young person's life by attempting to replace what he missed
growing up—an example of Christ's love for his church—the
Christian home.

Conclusion

During the sixties, the country was shocked into the reality of a very dissatisfied, vocal campus community. Broken windows, gutted buildings, and locked-up officials were common on campuses throughout the country. Somehow the Christian community develops spurts of motivation to reach people when that particular group displays open defiance against the American system. The reaction to the campus riots was the revival of campus ministries and the publication of scores of books on Christian apologetics. The subtle implication of such a reaction is that God is trying to preserve the system, and salvation is only applicable as it keeps people in their place. This is a cheap motivation for such a big need. Sin is in the heart. Dissension and immorality are the result of a man's separation from a righteous God. To the student, Christ must be portrayed as an answer to the perplexing questions of life.

For the most part, collegiates have rejected the church, not Christ or religion. Numerous student-led Christian movements are sweeping the campuses, but are not identifying themselves with the local church and in some cases are unashamedly speaking out against it. The Jesus Movement of the early seventies was evidence of the great spiritual needs of campus life. Presently, students are converting to Christ at an increasing rate. The interest in religion, however, has not been limited to Christianity but to Eastern religions and Satanism as well.

The church must make a major effort to have relevant ministries on university campuses. The church must also be in support of campus ministers.

Effective discipleship is not a result of better programs, but of better disciple-makers. The attitudes and motives of the Christian community toward the collegiate must be one of love and patience.

The church is not a forgotten idea and college students are not impossible to reach. There can be an interdependent relationship between these distant relatives. This, however, will become a reality only when the church community practices the Great Commission as the disciples did in the early church.

Notes

1. Hollis Green, *Why Churches Die* (Minneapolis: Bethany Fellowship, 1972), p. 20.

2. Os Guinness, *The Dust of Death* (Downers Grove, Ill.: Inter-Varsity Press, 1973), p. 190.

10.
Incorporating Youth into the Church

Denny Rydberg

> incorporate . . . formed or combined into one body
> or unit; intimately united, joined, or blended.[1]

YOUTH. KIDS. TEENAGERS. Whatever term we use to describe
them, there's a lot of them living today. Over 28½ million teenagers live in the United States alone.[2] Some of them live with
parents who attend church. And some of them are even members of the church themselves.

As we older members of the church are prone to say, "Young
people are the church of the future." But they are also part of
the church today. The current generation of young people are
big, bright, informed, and articulate. They have a contribu-

DENNY RYDBERG is the editor of the *Wittenburg Door* and a con-
sultant with David C. Cook Publishing Co. He is the editor of a new
curriculum for young people entitled LifeStyle published by Cook. Mr.
Rydberg is a graduate of Seattle Pacific College and has done graduate
work in psychology at Western Washington State College. He is married
and has one daughter.

tion to make to the total church. But many of them can't.
They're discriminated against. They do not have a platform
from which to speak or a base from which to serve. They're not
incorporated into the lifeblood of the church. And that's the
focus of this chapter. Incorporating youth into the church. What
does it mean to incorporate youth into the church? And how
can it be done?

Is Involvement Incorporation?

How do we incorporate youth into the church?

Do we build a giant, gung-ho program that attracts kids and
encourages them to participate in the youth program? Maybe.

Do we place a young person on each committee of the church,
and encourage youth to share their ideas in local board meetings? Possibly.

Do we hire a music man who sets up a youth choir that performs on Sunday evenings? Do we have the teenagers teach
Sunday school, lead at midweek prayer services and pray aloud
in front of adults? Is this incorporation? Could be.

All of the above might be part of incorporation. But they
don't penetrate to the root of the problem. Incorporation doesn't
begin with a program, it begins with an attitude. Incorporating
youth into the church means that the young people are part of
the warp and woof of the church. They are intimately involved.
They are an integral part of the whole.

What the Youth Say

In preparation for this discussion, I talked personally with
young people from a variety of churches in California. I asked
them what it meant to be incorporated into the church. Here's
what they said incorporation means to them.

1. To be loved and accepted for who you are, not for who
   you will be someday.

2. To have a say in what goes on in the church (or at least in what goes on that you're interested in).
3. To have an important part in the ministry of the total church. To feel like you're making a contribution that matters.
4. To be ministered to. To have your own needs met. To feel like you have a pastor, a place to worship, and people to worship with. To have people and a pastor who care about you.

In October 1974, Archbishop John R. Quinn of Oklahoma City touched on some of these same issues when he spoke at the Fourth World Synod of Bishops (Roman Catholic) in Rome. James W. Reapsome, editor of *Youth Today,* summarized Quinn's message in the November 1974 issue.

1. The chief problem for many young people is not the gospel or Jesus Christ, but the church. They don't see "the light of Christ shining on the countenance of the church." This doesn't mean it isn't there, but they do not perceive it.
2. They reject attempts to reach them simply for their attendance at mass, or for their financial support. "They want to be reached for their own sake, for their own inherent worth, and not for some ulterior purpose, however good or holy."
3. They are looking for a model of Christ and the gospel in the lives of priests and bishops.
4. The qualities they want to see most are joy, love, kindness, patience, tolerance, an open mind, a willingness to listen, a spirit of compassion and concern, a sincere and honest simplicity, and directness.
5. The chief barrier is not primarily church structures, approaches, or methodologies. "It is chiefly the problem of the minister of the church who, rightly or wrongly, frequently does not reveal to them that Christ whom they find in the gospel."

Archbishop Quinn went on to explain how this problem develops in the Roman Catholic Church:

The only time many young people see a priest or bishop is at the liturgy. If they do not perceive in him on those occasions the qualities described above, and especially joy and a spirit of faith, they do not believe in the church. They frequently find that the liturgy is celebrated in an impersonal manner, without joy and without any really obvious faith on the part of the celebrant. This does not seem to them to reflect the gospel as they understand it. They recognize the paradox of the joyless herald of the good news and are repelled by it.

Apart from the liturgy, they look for these qualities in their personal contacts with priests and bishops. Presence and visibility of bishops in their world is most important to youth. They yearn for contact with the true ministers of Christ who clearly reflect to them the mind and heart of Christ.

They look for priests and bishops with whom they can identify. Such priests and bishops should have the qualities mentioned earlier, but they must also be like the Christ of the Epistle to the Hebrews, "encompassed by weakness." They are attracted to the Christ of the Gospels, not only because of his openness, kindness and compassion, but also because he comes across to them as one who had to struggle with challenges from within and from without, as they have to struggle.[3]

Quinn was speaking to Roman Catholics, but his words apply to all members of the church. If young people do not feel they are loved for who they are, desired for who they are, and ministered to for who they are, they will not feel incorporated into the church. And they will see no reason to be incorporated. The attitude on the part of church leaders and members towards youth is crucial and critical.

The Attitude of the Senior Pastor

Whether we approve of the situation or not, the senior pastor in the Protestant church is still the key person and determining force in the church. If the pastor is anti-youth, or indifferent to youth, or too busy for youth, incorporation may never take place.

In most churches, in my opinion, members take their cues from the pastor. The pastor, to a great extent, influences the spirit and attitude of a church. If the pastor is hard-nosed and highly critical, the church will likely project that image. If the pastor is open and interested in the quality of relationships, the church often becomes more open and relational over the years. If the pastor is into positive or possibility thinking, the majority of the people will be also.[4] And even if the pastor doesn't influence a particular congregation's spirit, it is still important for the youth of that church to see that the pastor—their pastor—does care for them and consider youth important.

Spiritual Superstars?

But let's get practical. What can the pastor and other interested adults do to project this attitude of acceptance and love?

First, adults can lead from a stance of warmth, humanness, and weakness. Youth are looking for warmth in the midst of cold reality. They're looking for real people with real problems in the real world. They are not necessarily looking for spiritual superstars. They are looking for people who are making their way in a complex, cluttered world.

We as adults should not be afraid to be honest. We need to share with youth where we're hurting, where we're healing, where we're succeeding, where we're failing, and what we're learning in the process.

But before we tell them all about us, we need to listen.

Keith J. Leenhouts, the judge from Royal Oak, Michigan, who started the successful Volunteers in Probation program writes, "Attitudes are not changed by platitudes. Human conduct is changed by human contact. People change people."[5]

And then Leenhouts describes a volunteer who learned the importance of listening in the process of human contact. "Rhett was learning the lesson every volunteer must learn. Who he is—

often a reasonably successful person—may speak so loudly that probationers—more often the unsuccessful in society—can't hear what the volunteer says until he has done two things for months: first, be there; second, listen." [6]

The normal relationships between adults and youth are not the same as those between a volunteer and a probationer in Leenhouts' program. But the dynamics of attitude change are the same. Even if we can't agree with, or can't identify with what's being said, we need to listen.

And if we feel so out of touch with youth that we don't even know where to begin in working on our attitudes, we should be honest and tell them. "I feel out of touch. But I'd like to get to know you better."

We need to treat the youth as we do the adults in the church. Respect them. Remember their names. Drop them a note if they do something well. Call on them when they're ill and don't just send the youth sponsor or youth director because the sick person is "in their group."

And if we really want to relate with youth, we need to open our homes to them. We don't have to do it every week, but occasionally we should invite the youth over for refreshments and a chance to rap. If we've never done it before, we might be prepared with some questions to ask them. But after a while, they'll have questions they'll want to ask us.

That's the beginning. The spiritual overseers, the pastor, the leaders set the tone—an attitude of equality, respect, and love for youth.

But let's not go overboard in our response to the extent that youth become the prima donnas in the church whose every whim is gratified because we don't want to lose "the church of the future." Equality means giving and taking and youth need to learn this. But if the attitude is right, learning without undue hostility and resentment can take place for both youth and adults.

Common Projects and Experiences

Attitudes can also be worked on on a larger scale by involving youth and adults in common projects or experiences.

Some practical suggestions:

1. *Don't age-group all Sunday school classes.* In the summer (or whatever time period you choose), change the pace. Have a series of electives that involve young people and adults. The give and take in a Sunday school class over a thirteen-week period can help various age groups see each other's points of view.

2. *Involve adults and youth in retreats and mission projects.* When Chuck Miller was youth pastor at Lake Avenue Congregational Church in Pasadena, he crossed generational lines with a series of weekend retreats. He took the same number of members from his college group and from the forty to forty-nine age bracket to spend a weekend together. Later he took an even mixture from the college-age group and from those in their fifties and sixties. These weekends gave all the participants a greater appreciation for the testimonies and life styles of each other, regardless of age.

Russ Cadle of Fourth Presbyterian Church in Washington, D.C., conducted youth retreats at the church. Housing for Saturday night was provided by different adults in the church. The youth did whatever the host family was accustomed to doing on Saturday night. The next day, the youth sat together in church with the host families and later participated in an Agape Feast where all the young people and all the host families ate a meal together. Results: Greater respect for youth and adults in the church. Improvement in attitudes. Aids to incorporation.

Then . . . the Program

After attitudes have been modified and improved, program follows. Incorporation connotes involvement. But the involvement of youth in the church should not be styled on performance. Youth Sundays where kids *present* a program *to* the adults is performance first and service second.

Young people should be encouraged and trained to teach younger children in the Sunday school. They should be encouraged and trained to be involved with adults in a ministry to the poor. They should be allowed to serve on official church boards where their words do have as much weight as those of the others. Participation in the regular worship service in Scripture reading, prayer, etc., should be encouraged. Young people should be allowed to be *equal,* but not *superior* or *extra-special.*

Incorporating Their Brains Out

A friend and I recently discussed the incorporation issue. In the course of conversation, he said, "Sometimes we incorporate their brains out." Roughly translated, it means that sometimes we overincorporate. We do this with youth and adults.

The purpose of the church is not to get all the Christians into a building on as many days of the week as possible. The church exists to equip the saints for ministry (Eph. 4:11–15). But if the youthful saints are always at the church attending programs, and serving on committees, they can easily be cut off from a ministry to their own culture at school, parties, games, etc.

And it's equally tragic to see youth overincorporated to the extent that they're so busy at church that they lose a sense of community at home. Let's incorporate youth into the church. But let's incorporate with a sense of priorities—priorities to home and ministry.

"There Is neither Youth nor Adult" (?)

"There is neither Jew nor Greek, there is neither slave nor free, there is neither male nor female; for you are all one in Christ Jesus." (Gal. 3:28, RSV).

That's biblical incorporation.

I only wish Paul had added the words, "There is neither youth nor adult." In our twentieth-century culture, we have a tendency in the church to discriminate on the basis of age. Senior citizens are shuffled off to the Golden Hours club. Youth are confined to the youth group.

But the New Testament does not discriminate on the basis of age. Jesus said, "Let the children come to me, and do not hinder them; for to such belongs the kingdom of heaven" (Matt. 19:14, RSV). And young people like Timothy and John Mark were used in key areas of the total church. God ministered *to* and used the services *of* young people.

Let us follow the example of our Master. Equality, not discrimination. Incorporation, not alienation.

Notes

1. *Webster's New World Dictionary* (Cleveland, Ohio: World Publishing Co., 1968).

2. *Statistical Abstract of the United States, 1974.*

3. James Reapsome, in *Youth Today* (Philadelphia: Evangelical Foundation, November 1974), p. 6.

4. For a personal reflection on this conclusion, visit First Baptist Church of Hammond, Indiana; First Presbyterian Church of Hollywood, California; and Garden Grove Community Church of Garden Grove, California.

5. Keith J. Leenhouts, *A Father . . . a Son . . . and a Three Mile Run* (Grand Rapids: Zondervan, 1975), p. 85.

6. Ibid., pp. 132–33.

11.
A Christian Life Style for Singles

Lyle Hillegas

IT WOULD SEEM obvious that in thinking through and carrying out a life style, a single Christian person would give first place to biblical considerations. It is my observation, however, that while many Christian single persons desire this, they often instead get caught up in the mold of our secular perspective. I see a number of reasons for this.

But first let me say that much of what follows arises from personal observation and experience, and thus is presented from a male point of view. The use of masculine pronouns, however, is not meant to be discriminatory but is merely for convenience.

Hindrances to a Christian Life Style

There are many hindrances to finding and living a Christian life style which are common to all Christians, whatever their

LYLE HILLEGAS is president of Westmont College, Santa Barbara, California. He is a graduate of Bryan College, Dayton, Tenn., and has the Th.D. degree in church history from Dallas Theological Seminary. He has done postgraduate work at North Texas State, Michigan State, and Cambridge University. Before becoming president he was associate professor of religious studies at Westmont.

marital status. But as a single person, I have found four in particular that keep singles from being effective Christians.

1. A deep concern and preoccupation with his/her single status.

A preoccupation with one's singleness is prompted from forces without and within a person. Society in general usually doesn't allow a single person to forget his status. The only conclusion that can possibly be drawn from a majority of the responses elicited when a person's singleness is announced (and with men, anyway, it is usually publicly announced) is that singleness is abnormal or at best temporary. People tend to wonder why a person is still single after he has reached marriageable age, and their questions run the gamut:

- Is he too immature to face up to the responsibilities of marriage?
- Is he too unsure of himself (poor self-image)?
- Is he too promiscuous to restrict his sexual loyalties to one individual?
- Is his sexual orientation toward his own sex?

Almost never does anyone suggest that perhaps the person's single state is determined by dedication to a task that has preempted marriage, or by preference for a single life for whatever reason. Since almost everyone asks the questions I've mentioned, the single person who may already be troubled with the truth or the feared truth of the answers to those questions for himself becomes even more frustrated.

2. A tendency to procrastinate in doing anything significant until one is married.

A single person is often so determined that marriage is essential to his wholeness that subconsciously he bypasses both opportunities and responsibilities until they can be shared with a life partner. More seriously, this tendency to wait for the future can become a living pattern, canceling out many enriching experiences.

3. A growing pattern of going it alone.

Sometimes in an effort to overcorrect an image of single ir-responsibility, there is a strong urgency to hack out life's problems single-handedly. While just praise is due for personal initiative and discipline, one of the basic truths related to the Body of Christ is the fact that we can't make it on our own. But the single person has no one who is committed to him for the rest of his life, who will hang in there regardless of the rough waters, and thus he uniquely becomes a prey to the Enemy's traps. Many of the temptations he faces relate to areas shared only in deep relationships, and for many singles there simply is no one who has offered that kind of friendship. In quiet desperation he tries to fight on—many times lonely and afraid—afraid that he really can't make it by himself.

4. A tendency toward more and more selfishness.

Since no other human being really has to be taken into consideration in most of his life-planning, the single person can develop a pattern of self-orientation. There is no one else to spend his money on, no one to check with in making plans, so he seeks only those situations that bring the most satisfaction, avoiding that which is negative and might be related to ministry partly on the premise that life is already hard enough as a single person—who would choose to make it any more difficult? The result can be almost total self-seeking without intending it or realizing it. And so the single person is unknowingly caught in a web which is not planned but that rather automatically takes over as a result of the self-seeking influence of a secular society.

How to Have a Christian Life Style

But there are avenues to a godly perspective and some means to Christ-honoring ends in the life of a single person who desires to be obedient and seriously pursues that end. I see a number of factors as imperative in achieving that end.

1. Recognizing that the call to godly living is as real to the single person as to anyone else.

Those of us who are single look to the same source for life instruction as does the rest of society. There is no special revelation for single people. And the basic challenge to all, it seems to me, is a challenge to see our role as lovers in a love-starved world—lovers of God and then of our neighbors. That is, we recognize who our Creator is and then give ourselves to his service, which leads us to a recognition of the value of our neighbors as we then seek their welfare.

Thus, singles are *first called* to be lovers. This means that we are perceivers of the right hierarchy of values—God first, then other persons. It means that we are servants, since love is meaningless without a servant attitude.

The process of opening oneself up to this reality can be accomplished only through a welcoming attitude toward the Holy Spirit to create and encourage in us his fruit. Here is where we begin.

2. Opening up to God's sovereign work in our lives without bitterness.

We need to be open to what God is doing in our lives, and accept both what seems good and what seems bad. Two dangers persist here. First, there is the danger which belongs to all the human race of failing to bow before a sovereign God who has rightful claim in our lives. Second, a single person experiences the special danger of locking out all negative and demanding experiences and failing to recognize them as a part of what God is trying to do in forming his character in our lives. The single person can more totally lock out people and experiences that seem undesirable than those who have family relationships. All you have to say is "I already have plans," and you're out of anything you wish to avoid. You think you can sovereignly regulate all the circumstances of life until an invasion of people or events is permitted by Providence—and this can be doubly resented.

3. Committing oneself to constant review of the Scriptures as a perspective corrective.

We are barraged by thousands of messages all day, every day, most of which do not have the perspective of revelation, and we need a daily corrective on the nature of reality at the following levels:

- A sovereign loving God *does* exist and we are not alone in the universe—there is a purpose and plan at work.
- Forgiveness is a possibility, thus posing the real potential for a fresh start.
- Human nature can change, and God is enthusiastic about that positive change.
- My brother and sister are more like God than anything else I will ever contact. They are both valuable and eternal.
- Service—the costly giving of myself—is the essence of life and, therefore, to be entered into willingly and even eagerly.

This message comes through to me only in the Scriptures and is demonstrated to me by my brothers and sisters. I need *daily* reminding and even then don't do too well.

4. Binding oneself to others because it seems they have been brought into my life providentially and I can somehow productively feed into their lives.

I feel strongly that God does bring into our lives those to whom he would have us minister (not always of our choosing) and that these people are our special responsibility for as long as he chooses. Here the real test of ministry and love is experienced.

5. Working on at least one very deep and satisfying relationship.

We must allow someone to enter our lives at a very significant and personal level so that the burdens of life can be shared and prayed about, and a genuine caring grows between us and the other person. These are "given" things and must begin with prayer. They are very precious and mean the difference between making it and not making it.

*6. Finding a relationship with commitment to a group which
is part of the church.*

There is no substitute for belonging to a group of fellow
believers in a strong enough way so that one feels responsible
to these people—strong enough so that other plans are adjusted
in favor of these brothers and sisters. It is my strong conviction
that single people need to make an effort at this point to be
related to married people and their families. As difficult as this
may seem, entrance into family relationships in a give-and-take
way is a lifeline to be seriously sought. The context of home,
husband, wife and children bring to single life an element of
reality that must be embraced if at all possible. Families and
single persons need to see the challenge of this relationship and
work hard at putting the possibility to work.

*7. Recognizing the measure of freedom held, and con-
sciously harnessing that privilege to productive use.*

If conscious dedication of single freedom is by-passed, resentment toward intrusion of that freedom is the most likely
result. Here, the single person is called upon to understand his
personal gifts as clearly as possible, to come to an understanding of his responsibility in the context of the opportunities in
his life, and to move aggressively as he understands God's will
in regard to the use of his time, energies and resources. Without
this conscious move, life easily sifts through his fingers and no
sense of mission occurs.

Freedom is not something to be carefully caressed for its own
sake, but a resource to be put to work. If we are Christ's, it
means determining to pour ourselves out in the arena to which
each of us is personally called.

Freedom saved becomes a monster which refuses to be har-
nessed in any end other than personal gratification. The ugliness
of life which results is something all of us have known in some
measure—and have found unsatisfying.

The details of all these principles must be worked out with
wonderful variety in individual lives. If they are applied, I be-

lieve those of us who are single will find ourselves thrust beyond the shackles of self-centered existence to lives of effective
service which will result in the thrill of having influenced others'
lives as effective change agents. That makes single life exciting
and worthwhile—as it should be.

Study Guide

Gary R. Collins

THE PURPOSE of a study guide is to help individuals or groups of readers better understand, evaluate and interact with the ideas that are presented in a book or collection of articles. The chapters which comprise the preceding pages contain a number of insights and sometimes conflicting opinions, written by capable people who have given serious thought to what it means to be single. By adding a study guide, it is hoped that you will be encouraged and helped to think back over what has been written and to arrive at some further conclusions of your own.

It is possible, of course, to work through this study guide on your own but you might find group discussion to be more beneficial and interesting. The following study guide has been designed, therefore, for individual study which leads to group interaction. Whenever a group meets, there should be a leader who can guide the discussion and stimulate interaction. The same leader can direct all of the discussions, or you may want to shift leadership responsibilities so that a different person, chosen from the group, leads each of the sessions.

Before meeting, each group member should read the chapter or chapters to be discussed, complete the preparation assignments, and look over the questions which follow. These questions are designed to stimulate discussion and at times may lead to lively debate. The leader should encourage everyone to express his or her views, should maintain a somewhat objective perspective in the group, and should try to keep the discussion from getting too far off the track. When there are irreconcilable differences, the leader should have the right to stop discussion until more homework can be done, expert advice can be obtained, or the group agrees that discussion has reached a dead end.

One final comment: the questions and exercises which follow are merely suggestive. If you can think of questions which are better, use them. It might be more fun that way!

Chapter 1: Nancy Hardesty
Being Single in Today's World

Preparation

1. As you read the chapter by Nancy Hardesty, ask yourself, "With what do I agree and with what do I disagree?" Take notes on your reactions for discussion in the group.

2. Hardesty makes several references to the Bible. Look up the following and ask yourself what, if anything, each of these has to do with singleness.

> Proverbs 18:22
> Proverbs 21:9
> Ecclesiastes 4:9–12
> 1 Corinthians 7:8, 9
> 1 Corinthians 7:32–35

Meeting Together

3. To get started, the group members (including the leader) should introduce themselves. Indicate why you are in this discussion group.

4. If this has not been clarified previously, decide how often you will meet, for what length of time, what topics will be discussed each week and how the leadership responsibilities will be handled. Will the same person always be leader or will leadership responsibilities rotate between group members?

5. What are your reactions to Hardesty's chapter?

6. One critic has suggested that Hardesty writes "more from personal bias than from an objective study of the Bible." Do you agree or disagree? Give reasons for your answers. (At this point you

might want to share what you wrote under question 2 in the preparation section above.)

7. Near the end of her chapter Hardesty lists nine concluding
points about the single life. Look at these carefully. Do you agree
that "our home is the church, our family the body of believers"?
What implications does this have for single people? What are the
implications for married people?

8. Look at the conclusion beginning "our thinking about closeness
and touch should be concrete, contemporary . . . " What are the
practical implications of this for single people?

9. In her chapter, Hardesty refers to Genesis 2:18 and asserts
that "it is not marriage which is essential" for intimacy. How does
this relate to the context of Genesis 2 (see especially verses 22–25)?
Are there better passages of the Bible for supporting singleness as
a viable life style?

10. What can we conclude about singleness through the discussion of Hardesty's chapter? List the group conclusions.

Chapter 2: Linda LeSourd
Living Creatively: The Single Woman and the Church

Preparation

1. Linda LeSourd's chapter is addressed to two basic issues:
how the church can minister to singles and how singles can minister
within the church. Although the chapter concerns the single woman,
almost everything that the author says about women could also be
true of single men. As you read the chapter, try to decide in what
specific and practical ways the church can meet the needs of singles.

2. Turn to Romans 12. This is not addressed to singles necessarily but it could be a blueprint for the role of the single person in
the church. What are some practical teachings from this chapter
that could guide the single person as he or she participates in the
church?

Meeting Together

3. LeSourd argues that the church "lifts and heralds marriage as

the highest, noblest life style." Is this an accurate statement? If so, how can people in the church, both married and single, be helped to change their opinion?

4. Do you agree with the author that a single person's need for love, security and deep relationships with others can be met effectively outside of marriage? How should this be done? Do such relationships help the individual to "adjust creatively to singleness" as LeSourd contends?

5. The chapter is somewhat critical of singles groups within the church. What is your opinion of such groups? Would you agree that it is better for singles to be involved in the total church community where they can enjoy the diversity of the whole Body of Christ? What are the practical implications of this for your church?

6. The author identifies two schools of thought about the role of women in the church. Describe each of these. With which are you more in agreement? Why? Give biblical reasons for your opinions. Keep the discussion focused on singles.

7. "The church today is in danger of losing the involvement of the single woman (or man) because its family emphasis, program orientation and separation of singles leaves her (or his) needs unmet." What can the church do to avoid this danger and really minister to singles? List the suggestions of your group.

Chapter 3: Mark Lee
The Church and the Unmarried

Preparation

1. In this chapter, Mark Lee offers some reasons why people remain single. If you are single, list some reasons why you are single. If you are married, give the reasons for your decision not to be single. Give this careful thought and try to be honest with yourself.

2. Turn now to Matthew 19, the scripture that was mentioned in this chapter. Read verses 1–12. Do you get the impression here that marriage is pictured as a potentially difficult relationship? Does

Jesus imply that singleness is better? Look once again at 1 Corinthians 7:8–9.

Meeting Together

3. Jesus, Paul, Mary, Martha, and a number of other men and women in the New Testament appear to have been single. How would they have been received in your church? Do you agree that single people are looked down upon by those who are married? How should singles react to this implication that to be single is to be "selfish, excessively affluent, sex-oriented, and irresponsible"? What should married people do about such prejudices?

4. Lee mentions some of the frustrations or disadvantages of being single. He also mentions some advantages. Make a list of these advantages of being single and list the frustrations that single people face. How can these frustrations be dealt with in a practical way?

Advantages	*Frustrations*	*Dealing with Frustrations*

5. Near the end of his chapter, Lee identifies four attitudes that singles have towards their own potential marriage. What are these? Do you agree that most singles fit into one of these categories? What are the advantages and disadvantages of each?

6. Lee openly discusses the issue of sex and the single person. What are the sexual stresses that singles face? How can the Christian single person deal with these? Try to be honest and specific in answering these questions. Your group may wish to divide into smaller groups to discuss this important issue.

7. Seven suggestions are made in this chapter to enable the church to minister more effectively to singles. Discuss each of these suggestions. Are they feasible? What others should be added? How can each of these be brought into your church to change its ministry to singles? What is your plan of action for bringing about these changes? Record the group's specific practical suggestions.

Chapter 4: Virginia McIver
Learning to Live Alone: The Divorced Person and the Church

Preparation

1. What do you think about divorced people? Be honest! How you act towards divorced people is a pretty good indicator of your attitudes towards them. In the first column below write your attitudes towards divorced people. In the second column write what your attitudes should be. Use a separate sheet of paper if necessary.

My Attitudes	*Attitudes I Should Have*

2. Turn to Matthew 19, the passage we considered with chapter 3. Read verses 1–9 What is Jesus' teaching on divorce?

Meeting Together

3. In her warm and revealing chapter, McIver identifies some of the unique needs of divorced people. What are these needs? How do the needs of the divorced differ from those of persons who have never married? Do divorced men have needs that differ from divorced women?

4. Writing in a national magazine, a Christian psychiatrist recently argued that "divorce is never necessary." Do you agree? Look again at Matthew 19. Would Jesus have agreed that divorce is never necessary?

5. Divorced people sometimes face ostracism and rejection in the church. Is this true of your church? What should be the church's attitude towards the divorced?

6. McIver points out that "just because you are divorced does not mean you are no longer qualified to serve" in the total life of the church. How do you respond to this statement? Some would main-

tain that 1 Timothy 3 (especially verses 1–5, 7, 11–12) bans divorced people from leadership in the church. Do you agree? Give reasons for your answer.

7. Is it true that "the greatest need and the one most neglected in the church is a ministry to a couple when they are separated, facing divorce, and making adjustments during the time immediately after"? If so, how can the church work to deal with this neglected aspect of the ministry?

8. In her own case, McIver was helped "not by 'the church' but by people in the church." List some specific things that you as individuals can do and are doing to help divorced persons and those facing divorce. Summarize the group answers to this question.

Chapter 5: Britton Wood
The Church's New Frontier

Preparation

1. "The people of God are on the edge of one of the greatest adventures the church has ever known." According to Wood, what is this adventure? Think about its implications for your church and your own life.

2. How might each of the following apply to divorce?
   Matthew 5:31–32
   1 John 1:9
   Matthew 7:1–5
   Galatians 6:1–2
   Ephesians 4:31–32
   Ephesians 6:18

Meeting Together

3. If there are divorced persons in your group or if an outsider is willing to join the group for one session, you might want to begin with the dialogue suggested by Wood in his chapter. In this, the formerly married are invited to state "what I wish someone had told me before I married (assuming I would have listened)." Married

couples and the widowed, as well as divorced persons, could also give input to this discussion. How could the information from this discussion help (a) your church, (b) the unmarried, (c) the married, and (d) you personally?

4. Wood suggests that "it's O.K. to be a single adult today." In your church and community is it O.K. to be divorced? Why or why not?

5. The chapter lists five difficulties that the church faces in ministering to single people, especially those who are divorced. How can each of these be overcome, especially in your church?

6. Wood lists six concerns of the formerly married. Is this list accurate? Is it complete?

7. How do you react to Wood's suggestions that:
- divorced persons often are made to feel guilty in the church?
- many married adults show a superior attitude in relating to the divorced?
- married people sometimes are threatened by divorced people?
- legal divorce may occur long before it is emotionally accepted by the divorced individual?
- single people in the church often feel a "pressure to marry as life's only fulfillment option"?
- the church is the best avenue of help and health for the formerly married?

8. At the conclusion of the chapter, the author gives eight practical guidelines for a church ministry to the formerly married. Evaluate each of these suggestions. As stated in his chapter, Wood has about eight hundred single people in his church. Would the guidelines in this chapter apply to a church with only a few singles? Decide on practical ways by which your church can minister to the divorced. Write out some specific suggestions. What is your plan for putting these ideas into practice?

Chapter 6: Joan Salmon Campbell
Handling Grief: The Widow and the Church

Preparation

1. How do you feel when you are in the presence of someone who has recently lost a mate? Are you uncomfortable, not sure what to say, inclined to be doing things for the bereaved, fearful? At the beginning of her widowhood, Joan Salmon Campbell found it difficult to "endure" the bemoaning attitudes and "intended kindness" of those church members who came to help and offer condolences. This chapter can stimulate us to think through our attitudes to widowhood and the needs of men and women who are single because of the death of a mate.

2. James 1:27 and 1 Timothy 5:4–16 make reference to widows. As you read these passages, try to decide what should be the church's responsibility to widows and widowers. What should be your responsibility as an individual?

Meeting Together

3. Campbell's chapter has some interesting insights into death and grief from the widow's point of view. Have you thought about your own death? Who would grieve? Do single people and married persons view and face death in different ways? If so, what are the differences?

4. Divorce and the death of a spouse both involve the end of a marriage and a return to the single state. In what ways does the widowed person's readjustment differ from that of the divorced person?

5. Campbell lists four ways in which the single person and the church can "nurture each other." What are these four suggestions? Can you think of others?

6. What can the widowed person do to readjust smoothly to being a single person?

7. How can the church most effectively minister to the widowed both immediately after the spouse's death and in the months which follow? Try to be specific and practical in your answers.

Chapter 7: Robert Pinder
The Single-Parent Family and the Church

Preparation

1. Look at the last two sentences of Robert Pinder's chapter. Do you agree or disagree? Why?

2. Can you think of any single-parent families in the Bible? How did they get along? Look up James 1:27, Psalm 146:9. Do these have any relevance for single-parent families?

Meeting Together

3. What are the unique needs and stresses of the one-parent family? Does the single parent have problems and/or advantages that other singles do not have? What are these?

4. Is it possible for a married couple to live together but for only one parent to raise the children because of neglect, disinterest, or inability of the other parent? As he or she raises the children, in what ways is this parent similar to the parent whose spouse is gone? How can this one-parent family (with both parents present) be helped?

5. In his chapter, Pinder describes three stages of development: dependence (childhood), independence (presumably in adolescence and early adulthood) and interdependence. Does this theory have any practical relevance to the needs and problems of the single parent?

6. "When children are victimized, they feel helpless to take responsibility for their own lives and direction." Could this statement also apply to the parent who is left to raise children alone? How can both parent and child overcome the feeling of being victimized and help themselves (independently and together) to "take responsibility for their own life and direction"?

7. Do you agree that "single parents are generally the best ones for reaching out to other single parents"? Do you favor the formation of Christian "parents without partners" groups? How do you react to the suggestion that single parents should be integrated into the family life of the church and put into contact with both married and single adults in the congregation? How could this be done?

8. In what practical ways can you and your church minister to single parents and their children? Write out your specific suggestions. How do you plan to implement these guidelines?

Chapter 8: Barbara Sroka
Bridging the Gap: College Students and the Church

Preparation

1. Barbara Sroka's chapter gives a vivid and insightful picture of modern college students—most of whom are single. Notice, however, that much of what Sroka writes about college students applies equally to singles in general. As you read, think about ways in which the needs of students are both similar to and different from the needs of singles who are not in college.

2. Students are involved in study—an activity which the Bible heartily endorses. Look up 2 Timothy 2:14–17. Does this have relevance to the student, single or married?

Meeting Together

3. In her chapter, Sroka contrasts the Christian college with the secular college and identifies the problems which students face in each of these environments. Do you agree with the descriptions? How would you respond to the suggestion that "the basic difference between Christian college students and Christian students on secular campuses is that those on secular campuses have had their faith questioned and put to the test"? Would the statement be accurate if you started the sentence as follows: the basic difference between singles working for Christian organizations and singles who are in the secular world is . . . ?

4. What does Sroka mean by the "student posture"? Is there such a thing? Is there a "single posture"? If so, what bearing does this have on the single adult?

5. This chapter identifies several "generalizations" about college students. What are these? Would you change the list in any way?

How would you alter the list to include generalizations about single adults in general?

6. Now look at the chapter's listing of student needs. Discuss each of these needs, indicating (a) whether or not you have these needs personally, (b) how these needs can be met in your life and in the lives of others. Write out some specific ways in which student needs can be met by you personally and by your church.

7. Near the end of this chapter, Sroka mentions some reasons why students don't go to church. Could these also be reasons why singles don't go to church? Is the church "college-career group" a way to solve this problem? What are other alternatives?

Chapter 9: Rich Berry
The Church Cares for the College Student

Preparation

1. Rich Berry's chapter points to a very important topic for single and married Christians alike—the issue of discipleship. Since this is a book on singles, ask yourself how single people can do their part to fulfill the great commission (Matt. 28:18–20), how singles can be disciples and how they can disciple others. As you ponder this, remember that Jesus, probably the Apostle Paul, and at least some of the disciples were unmarried.

2. The following Scripture portions all mention discipleship. How might each apply to unmarried Christians?

>   John 13:34–35
>   John 15:8
>   Luke 14:25–26
>   Luke 14:27
>   Luke 14:33

Meeting Together

3. In this chapter the author discusses both personal evangelism and social involvement. What is the single person's responsibility in

these areas? Try to give practical and specific answers.

4. Is the quote from 1 Corinthians 9:22 of practical relevance to singles? How would you respond to the following adaptation of four sentences from Berry's chapter? "The Christian community must view the world around not as some place to visit and do evangelism and then leave, to come back to the sanctuary. Singles, particularly those away from home, are looking for relationships, not affiliations. . . . Presently, social involvement on the part of the evangelical church is still low on the list of priorities. By such lack of action on the behalf of equality and justice, the church has failed to communicate the idea that Jesus was neither communist nor capitalist, on the Right or on the Left, but acting in behalf of all peoples, all races, all political persuasions."

5. Berry points to the need for young Christians to be discipled. What does it mean to "make disciples" of others following their conversion? How is this done?

6. In his discussion of the home, the author indicates that "the biggest need among these college students is one of reaffirmation." In this sentence, could "singles" be put in the place of "college students"? How do we reaffirm and build up one another without appearing phony? In what specific ways can you reaffirm the people around you? Do you think this has anything to do with discipleship? Summarize the group discussion.

Chapter 10: Denny Rydberg
Incorporating Youth into the Church

Preparation

1. What is a chapter on youth doing in a book on singles? At first it doesn't seem to fit, until we remember that the 28½ million teens mentioned in Denny Rydberg's chapter are mostly single. Many of these kids feel as "left out" as do their older brothers and sisters who are single. In reading this chapter, ask yourself in what ways the problems of teenagers parallel those of single adults.

2. Timothy was probably young and single when he met Paul the apostle. Can we learn anything about young singles from the following?

    2 Timothy 1:5–6
    1 Timothy 4:12–16
    2 Timothy 2:2
    2 Timothy 2:22

Meeting Together

3. "Incorporating youth into the church means that the young people are part of the warp and woof of the church. They are intimately involved. They are an integral part of the whole." Could "singles" be substituted for "youth" and "young people" in the above quotation from Rydberg's chapter? How can singles, young and old, be incorporated into the church? What do you think of the suggestions that came from Rydberg's talks with the young people in California?

4. Do you think Archbishop Quinn's five points apply to Protestant churches as well as to Catholic churches? How does the church face the issues he raises? How can young singles be "loved for who they are, desired for who they are, and ministered to for who they are"?

5. Rydberg suggests that the church's ministry to youth begins with attitudes and experiences and is followed by programs. How do you react to this suggestion?

6. Read Acts 16:1–5. Timothy (a single young person) was taken under the wing of Paul (a single young adult). How can older singles help younger singles today? Is there danger of other persons being critical of an older-younger arrangement? What can be done to meet suspicions that the older single might have homosexual interests in the younger person?

7. Rydberg concludes his chapter with a reference to Galatians 3:28. Do you think it would be consistent with the rest of Scripture to conclude "There is neither Jew nor Greek, there is neither slave nor free, there is neither male nor female, there is neither youth nor adult, there is neither married nor single; for all are one in Christ

Jesus"? What are the implications of this for your church? What are the implications for you? Summarize the group discussion.

Chapter 11: Lyle Hillegas
A Christian Life Style for Singles

Preparation

1. This concluding chapter by Lyle Hillegas identifies a number of issues that single people should face as they develop a Christian life style. As you read, keep asking "How does this apply to me?"

2. The Apostle Paul had a very fulfilling life style. Turn again to 1 Corinthians 7:25–35, 39–40 and read his conclusions about marriage, singleness and the Christian life. How do you react to this? Does it have personal application to the way in which you live?

Meeting Together

3. Begin the discussion by thinking back over the entire book. What problems or challenges of being single have not been discussed in this book? How can these be dealt with in practical ways?

4. According to Hillegas, if you are single, then other people begin to think there must be something wrong: you must be immature, unsure of yourself, or sexually abnormal. How do you respond to this observation? Earlier in the book we discussed prejudice towards singles. Now that you have read the book do you have additional suggestions concerning how this prejudice against singles can be broken down?

5. In the first part of his chapter, Hillegas lists four attitudes commonly held by the unmarried. Do you agree with the author that these are common attitudes? Do you hold any of these yourself? What would you add to this list? Are these attitudes harmful? If so, how can they be changed?

6. To achieve a Christ-honoring life style for singles, the author lists seven guidelines which "must be worked out with wonderful variety in individual lives." What are these guidelines? Should any-

thing be added? How can these principles be "worked out" in your life? Be specific in your answer.

7. Near the end of his chapter, Hillegas writes that "the single person is called upon to understand his personal gifts as clearly as possible, to come to an understanding of his responsibility in the context of the opportunities in his life, and to move aggressively as he understands God's will in regard to the use of his time, energies and resources." What does this mean for singles in general? What does this mean for you? Write out how you plan to change your "Christian life style" in the immediate future. Be specific.

Selected Reading List

In addition to the books mentioned at the end of Nancy Hardesty's and Virginia McIver's chapters, here are some further titles for additional reading.

Andrews, Gini. *Sons of Freedom.* Grand Rapids: Zondervan, 1975.
——. *Your Half of the Apple: God and the Single Girl.* Grand Rapids: Zondervan, 1973.
Bel Geddes, Joan. *How to Parent Alone: A Guide for Single Parents.* New York: Seabury, 1974.
Jepson, Sarah. *Devotions for the Single Set.* Carol Stream, Illinois: Creation House, 1972.
——. *For the Love of Singles.* Carol Stream, Illinois: Creation House, 1970.
Law, Virginia. *As Far as I Can Step.* Waco, Texas: Word Books, 1970.
Lewis, C. S. *A Grief Observed.* New York: Seabury, 1963.
Marshall, Catherine. *To Live Again.* New York: McGraw-Hill, 1957.
McGinnis, Marilyn. *Single.* Old Tappan, New Jersey: Fleming H. Revell, 1974.
Mumaw, Evelyn K. *Woman Alone.* Scottdale, Pennsylvania: Herald Press, 1970.

Tompkins, Iverna. *How to Be Happy in No Man's Land.* Plainfield, New Jersey: Logos, 1975.

Towns, Elmer. *The Single Adult and the Church.* Glendale, California: Regal, 1967.